RETURNING TO STUDY

DUNDEE

University Library

RETURNING TO STUDY

A guide for professionals

Stuart Powell

Open University Press
Buckingham · Philadelphia

Open University Press
Celtic Court
22 Ballmoor
Buckingham
MK18 1XW

email: enquiries@openup.co.uk
world wide web: http://www.openup.co.uk

and
325 Chestnut Street
Philadelphia, PA 19106, USA

First Published 1999
Reprinted 2000, 2002

A catalogue record of this book is available from the British Library

ISBN   0 335 20131 8 (pb)   0 335 20132 6 (hb)

Library of Congress Cataloging-in-Publication Data
Powell, Stuart, 1949–
    Returning to study: a guide for professionals/Stuart Powell,
    p. cm.
    Includes bibliographical references (p.) and index.
    ISBN 0-335-20132-6. – ISBN 0-335-20131-8 (pbk.)
    1. Adult education – Great Britain.   2. Education, Higher – Great
Britain.   3. Continuing education – Great Britain.   4. Report
writing.   I. Title
LC5256.G7P66   1999
374′.941 – dc21   98–50319
                                                                               CIP

Typeset by Graphicraft Limited, Hong Kong
Printed in Great Britain by St Edmundsbury Press Ltd,
Bury St Edmunds, Suffolk

Dedicated to Edith and Les Powell

Contents

Preface

Returning to study as an adult learner can be a daunting and intimidating experience. However, it need not be so; the aim of this book is to help you make the most of your course of study, to balance the difficult juggling act of study, work, leisure and family life, and to draw upon insights and experience from your professional life to support your academic work.

In writing this book, I have tried to take account of the wide range of academic courses and differing professional backgrounds of readers and to offer practical and workable strategies which will be of value to you regardless of your particular discipline of study. The strategies have been tried and tested by professional students undertaking a variety of different courses. In the book you will find boxes containing issues for reflection and specific tasks. Some of these are supported by responses from students from a variety of backgrounds. I should add at this point that I have used the term 'client' throughout the book and in so doing intended to encompass the wide range of people who are in one way or another recipients of your professionalism. I include in this notion: customers, school children, patients, prisoners, tutees and so on. Also, you will notice that in the book I do not define overtly what I mean by 'professional'. While this may seem a serious omission I did not wish to be confined by a strict definition that might exclude some relevant issues for some people. Again,

I have taken a broad, inclusive view and have interpreted the matter of relevance as something for you as the reader to identify in terms of your own working situation. You may be interested to know that I write from experience of returning to study myself. While working as a primary school headteacher, I returned to university to study for a degree in education. Attempting to come to terms with the demands of academic work and to combine these with the pressures of a busy professional life and a typically hectic home environment gave me a keen insight into the difficulties which most professionals face when returning to study. However, most importantly, I also came to appreciate the joys and gains of study and to see how these translated into real benefits in both my professional and personal life. My aim in writing this book is to help you to minimize the difficulties and to reap the rewards of becoming a confident and enthusiastic learner.

The content of this book is also influenced by my work as a lecturer since entering higher education. I have been fortunate enough to work with postgraduate students, returning to study both part- and full-time, from every faculty. Through this work I have come to realize that, though different disciplines and professional backgrounds make different demands on students, common problems exist and similar solutions can be suggested. Finally, my own research has led me to two understandings which underpin this book: that a successful return to study in higher education requires critical reflection on the part of the student; and that success should be interpreted in terms of increased ability to think effectively as well as increased knowledge and skills.

Acknowledgements

I am grateful to Trevor Jones for his help in organizing the first pilot version of the document from which this book originated, to Janice Allen for her helpful comments on that document and to Claire Millward and Lucy Owen for their invaluable help in drawing together feedback from across the professions and for their useful comments on an early draft of the book. I am also grateful to all those students from various professional backgrounds who made anonymous comments on some of the ideas and tasks in this book. Finally, I would like to acknowledge all the students with whom I have had the pleasure of working over the years and whose experiences have informed the writing of this book.

1

Introduction

Some people study all their life and at their death they have learned everything except how to think.

(Domerque, quoted in Parnes *et al.*, 1977: 52)

Overview

It is important that you think about your reasons for returning to study and what you can and should expect from this new experience of learning before considering the particular strategies that may help you to function more effectively as a student in higher education. In this first chapter, we shall take it for granted that having good reasons for returning to study may sustain you if times become difficult, that one of the ways to get the most out of an experience of studying is to be as fully aware as possible of ways in which the very notion of learning can be interpreted and that when and where to study can be as important for the adult learner as some of the more detailed learning strategies. In this chapter therefore you will be asked to:

- identify your own reasons for returning to study and the implications of those reasons;
- examine your own interpretations of what counts as learning;
- think about questions of when and where to study.

Introduction

The quotation from Domerque at the head of this chapter suggests that a distinction can be drawn between the act of study and consequent learning and thinking. This chapter sets the scene for what follows in the book by suggesting that there is more to your successful return to study than simply finding ways of coping with a new kind of workload. Certainly the practicalities of how to go about study are important, but I hope to persuade you that a significant underlying purpose of your study is to improve your abilities as a thinker and hence as a potential learner in future situations. The accumulation of knowledge is one interpretation of learning but it is not the only one, and it may well be an interpretation that is confining rather than liberating.

Modern rhetoric calls for 'lifelong learning'; Domerque reminds us that such an endeavour is likely to remain sterile without improvement to the powers of thinking. You need to focus on your own ways of learning, your style as a thinker and your developing professional abilities.

Reasons for returning to study

Identifying reasons

My own reasons for returning to study related, as I recall, to a need to update and upgrade my professional qualifications and also to a feeling that I was missing something in terms of the depth of my understanding of what was going on in my professional work. On reflection, my initial professional training had not been as intellectually stimulating for me as it might have been (this is not to blame my tutors or the course I followed – the reasons were probably manifold, not least among them my own inclinations at the time). I recall vividly being uncertain of my own abilities second time around and trying to weigh curiosity (about my own abilities and about ideas) against possible difficulties and the potential embarrassment of low achievement and/or failure.

You will have your own reasons and possibly your own set of anxieties. Your reasons may be bound up with career advancement, or with a need to prove to yourself that 'you can do it', or with competition with colleagues, or it may be that your employer feels you need more qualifications. On the other hand, it may be that you have quite simply always wanted to engage in further study but have, for one reason or another, never had the chance.

It would be improper of me to impose my own view and suggest the kind of reason you should have for returning to study. Yet it has been a feature of discussions with students at the end of courses that they often mention, obliquely, self-improvement in terms of their own intellectual ability but seem embarrassed to come out and say that they think they have become a better or cleverer person. They do, however, sometimes admit to feeling more able to think clearly about issues, solve problems effectively, put across their views more accurately and confidently and so on. Whether or not you feel comfortable in anticipating such intellectual gain or are likely to lay claim to being improved in these terms at the end of your studies, the fact remains that study should improve the mind if it has any legitimate claim to success. Therefore it seems reasonable to suggest that 'learning how to think' is a possibility and might well be a part of your agenda (this topic is addressed in this book in the sections on critical thinking).

Whatever your reasons, returning to study, whether full-time or part-time, is by no means easy. Many students have pointed out to me, sometimes ruefully, that when they embarked on a course of study, perhaps for the first time in some years, the rest of life did not suddenly go on hold. Demands of work and family persist, and involvement in such things as hobbies and sports does not suddenly lessen in importance. But many students have found that, in the face of new and potentially conflicting demands, it helps to be clear about the reasons for accepting the challenge of further study. Indeed, identifying your reasons can lend a clear sense of purpose to new structures within your life and also create something to return to for reassurance if things do not quite go to plan.

Compensations

You may find that it is all too easy to lose sight of the compensations that can be gained from engaging in study when pressures mount and targets remain elusive. Identifying them for yourself at the outset is one way of ensuring that they, too, receive your attention. It should be said that the compensations will not necessarily be a matter of 'results' (grades and awards achieved and subsequent professional enhancement, for example); it may well be that new friends made and horizons broadened are also compensatory factors. Indeed, many students have commented upon how much their lives have changed in a positive sense because of their returning to university to study, and when I have pursued those remarks I have been surprised at the extent to which that positive change has been perceived by students to have occurred in their personal lives (this is not to say, of course, that there was not professional gain as well).

A useful text that explores the relationship between postgraduate study and lifelong learning and graduate employment is Burgess (1997).

Coping with guilt

Some of the students who gave feedback on an earlier version of this book noted that on their return to study they had experienced guilt as a result of having less time to spend with family and friends, and that it would be useful if I could describe ways to identify and cope with this kind of guilt. This presents something of a difficulty because I am not sure that there is any universal and straightforward way of going about it. What I might say as a tutor to one student would not necessarily be useful to another. However, it is worth pointing out that while your studies may seem to take up valuable time that you would usually spend in other areas of your personal and professional life, it may be the case that you will make more effective use of the time that you *are* able to spend in those areas. Also, there are likely to be benefits in terms of personal development resulting from your studies which will have positive knock-on effects for those around you.

I asked a range of returning students about any feelings of guilt that they might have. Their responses will hopefully convince you, if you do experience guilty feelings, that you are not alone.

I rationalize guilty feelings. These are generated by norms/
expectations of others/society. I usually know why I do
things.

(Nurse)

I feel no guilt at all about studying. If anything, I feel pride
as people benefit from my work.

(Medical engineer)

Of course I feel guilty about suddenly spending time shut
away in a room writing essays when I used to spend the
time with my family. But I try to compensate by making
the effort when I am with them. It works out OK, I think.

(Librarian)

Guilt is a harmful emotion but lack of it could indicate
failure to take account of the feelings of others (e.g. family).
I don't feel guilty because I have only pursued further
studies with the full support of my family.

(Psychologist)

I feel guilty at having to sacrifice doing other things for
people, e.g. mother. I feel guilty if I cannot do everything,
but there just is not time.

(Midwife)

'New' study and an existing lifestyle

It is quite likely that your way of living will have changed significantly since you last tackled the reading of set texts, the completion of practical assignments, the writing of essays and so on.
Indeed, returning students have told me that the prospect of
fitting in a whole new set of demands is one of the major concerns
that they have in the initial stages of returning to study. I should
add that a number of those same students have later reported
that what they initially thought of as a significant problem to
be overcome was, in reality, more a matter of readjustment and
manipulation of existing arrangements.

Changes in lifestyle

Inasmuch as your return to study will almost inevitably involve some change to your lifestyle, however minimal, then a first step to managing this is to identify your own characteristic way of living. Some events in your life are necessarily immovable (such as the time for collecting the children from school), while others are less precise in terms of timing but none the less necessary for life to go on (shopping for food). Effective change, which can be assumed to be that which involves a minimum of pain and the best use of your time and effort in new circumstances, then becomes a matter of thinking about how certain aspects of the way you live at present may end up being a barrier to study and identifying, realistically, what can be done about it. An important prerequisite to all of this is an acceptance on your part that some changes are necessary. This is a matter, in the first instance at least, of recognizing what can be changed and deciding what you want to change. You probably fulfil different functions in different aspects of your daily life, and hence behave differently in different spheres of activity – for example, unconsciously shifting from parent to boss to employee to son/daughter to counsellor to friend. Your becoming a student again is a matter, in this respect, of adopting a new functional role, of becoming something different for a new set of people.

Planning for study

In order to fit study into an existing lifestyle it may help if you raise your awareness of how your time is spent at present. Consider an average 24-hour day (accepting that the average day rarely happens). It may be useful to chart your main activities and then consider whether any of them need to be, and can be, adjusted if you are to complete your course of study successfully. Such charting can be done with a simple list, setting out the course of your typical day from the alarm clock going off to bedtime. On the other hand, you might prefer to attempt to represent your day diagrammatically using, for example, overlapping circles. In this way you could distinguish work from leisure or mark out different aspects within your work (e.g. practical tasks as opposed to the writing up of reports) or delineate time spent 'on task' and in travel.

The advantage of all this, of course, is that awareness of how time is spent may lead you to ways of controlling how you make use of the time that you have available. One of the students (a lawyer) who commented on some of the ideas in this book described the way in which he tried not to let studying time affect what he saw as the balance of his professional work by *'studying in "dead time", e.g. on train journeys, in waiting times and lunch breaks'*. A medical engineer who had returned to study after a number of years in his profession, described the way in which he carried out the computational side of his work during the day, because he did not have sufficient resources at home – in the evening he did his written work such as papers and reports. He recognized that the needs of the various tasks within his study programme to some extent drove the way in which he structured his day, and he acknowledged that the more he came to understand this the clearer his planning became. Clearly, then, having listed or drawn the outline of your daily schedule you still need to decide how to make the necessary adjustments, but at least now you may have a clearer view of what those adjustments are.

A recurring theme of discussions I have had with students about their own experiences of 'planning' in the initial stages of returning to study, is the importance of being clear about deadlines, typically for the handing in of assignments, and of planning backwards from them. My students have often found that the final stages of completing a piece of work for submission have taken longer than they had estimated; 'printing out' is traditionally a time for unexpected delay or disaster and subsequent angst (involving in one case an overwhelming need to be physically sick). Many students have also noted that work which is revisited after a period and corrected or updated before submission is invariably improved by the process. Indeed, later in this book I will discuss the importance of seeing the process of writing as a formative part of the development of your thinking about the topic in hand. Putting all of this together, it is clear that you should aim to finish work well before the deadline and thus allow for final amendments and possible distractions and difficulties.

Switching tasks and keeping track

Switching from one task to another may be a feature of life for you as a professional returning to study, in that work, home and study will inevitably impact on each other. However, there may also be a case for some planned switching between tasks. In terms of knowing yourself and your preferred learning style

 Task: Keeping track

What devices can you imagine being able to use to keep track of where you have got to with particular tasks (such as the writing of an assignment)?

 Student responses: How do you go about keeping track?

Personally I set myself milestones, such as that by a particular date I will have achieved the task I set out to do.

(Medical engineer)

I work on a word-processor and I always type a comment to myself at the start of a file to remind myself what I have done and what I was going to do next.

(Librarian)

I carry things in my head and write analytical memos which I don't refer to again.

(Nurse)

Self-evaluation of targets set by self, establish a work plan set by self, seek feedback from supervisor, have a research buddy to share work programmes and keep each other motivated and on task.

(Education consultant)

Diary on PC.

(IT technician)

and habits, it is useful to focus upon when you need to switch between activities to prevent boredom and lack of concentration. Deliberately switching from one activity to another may be a productive device for some people in some circumstances, but you may find it helpful to try to finish a previously defined step of a task before going on to something else. I find in my own work that returning to a task which was left 'in the air' means that I end up having to reorientate myself to the task; clearly this takes time which could have been more profitably used. It may be, of course, that you can devise ways of reminding yourself of just where you got to and what you were about to do (using coloured 'sticky notes' covered in self-directed comment is a common device).

The range of activities involved in study

One thing you can be sure about is that your studying will not be a matter simply of reading books, writing essays or carrying out experiments. The range of activities which you may need to engage in when 'studying' is illustrated by the list below:

- listening to lectures;
- asking questions and discussing issues with colleagues and fellow students;
- joining in seminar discussions;
- reading books, journal articles, technical reports, reviews;
- watching training videos;
- engaging in role play;
- writing notes and using them subsequently in the preparation of assignments;
- interviewing people;
- learning key ideas, deciding what is important and what is not;
- asking questions, deciding which questions have been useful and why;
- answering questions;
- preparing assignments;
- carrying out experimental work;
- preparing for written or oral examinations;

- reflecting on things learnt and on things that remain to be learnt;
- working out how people from different disciplines view problems in different ways;
- considering the effects of increased understanding on your professional practice or your personal life.

This list is not intended to be exhaustive, merely illustrative of the range of things that you may encounter in your studies. Neither is the list intended to be frightening; you should not feel daunted, but rather encouraged. Some returning students have reported that their initial view of study had been that it was all about writing essays (with, in some cases, the negative associations that this entailed) whereas they later came to realize that this had been to overstate the case. The point for us here is that different aspects of study will require different things of you in terms of time and place, as well as type and level of effort. We will return later in this book to many of the topics listed above.

Of course there is no substitute for hard work, but some of the short-cuts to making sure that the hard work you do is the right kind of hard work can be found in Race (1998).

Interpreting learning

Concepts of learning

What people value about learning, and the kinds of things they assume make someone a 'learned person', will vary over time and between cultures. In a Stone Age setting an understanding of the difference between poisonous and non-poisonous berries might be of vital significance and hence a valuable thing to learn. Things to be learnt, ways of learning them and ways of assessing them are not absolute and unchanging. My example of a Stone Age culture may seem a little extreme but it only extends what may be a reality for you, namely that if you have spent much time away from the world of academia or have crossed cultural boundaries then you may find that notions of what is deemed worthwhile knowledge, and what it is to study and to learn, have shifted. A clear example within current academic environments is that the memorizing of text and facts is valued in some contexts and cultures much more highly than it is in others (and indeed was valued within aspects of UK education of twenty years ago much more than it is today). Similarly, while the ability to remember facts may be seen as necessary for examination of learning at A level, at PhD level a candidate is usually permitted to take her/ his thesis into the oral examination and to refer to it when questioned, rather than expected to remember all that she/he wrote. Depending on your own circumstances, therefore, you need to be prepared for values to have shifted and to be on the lookout for signs (in course documentation and the attitudes of lecturers) that different kinds of knowledge and skills are being valued and different kinds of learning outcomes are therefore being targeted. Rowntree (1988) gives some invaluable insights into the different ways in which learning can be conceptualized and discusses the implications for study.

Professional awareness and competency

In considering different conceptions of learning we need to consider ways in which learning gains may occur for you as a professional. Wrapped up in the notion of being a professional is the idea that you will seek continuous self-improvement, learning more about your working environment and thereby becoming more effective within it. When you re-enter study, then, you may have an agenda which includes the idea that study is valuable inasmuch as it contributes to your own professional performance. In one sense I have no argument with this, but there may be a danger in expecting this value to be wholly transparent and direct. Professional work is necessarily multi-faceted and complex. It is not always a matter of what you know but of how well you are able to apply your knowledge in changing circumstances; it is not just that you have a defined battery of professional skills but also that you have the ability to convey to others how you are using those skills and what the effects are for them (be they fellow professionals or clients). For example, a vet needs to know what operation to perform as well as how to explain to the pet owner what the outcomes are likely to be and to give an assessment of risk versus potential gain. In short, just as professional effectiveness is hard to delineate and often hard to assess in a neat and tidy way (for example, my guess is that you are more likely to be 'appraised' than 'assessed'), so improvements in that effectiveness through study will be similarly hard to define and measure.

It is natural to have a legitimate expectation of professional gain from your return to study but it may be unwise to expect that gain to be clearly defined at the outset, apparent throughout and direct (in terms of specific learning leading to specific aspects of increased effectiveness). In particular, there may be a danger in the current climate, where it is commonplace to need to 'collect' so many modules for a particular qualification, that you risk losing sight of the underlying purpose of your return to study. My own experience of working with returning professional students and talking to them at points later in their careers has shown that many do indeed become more competent and more successful as a result of their return to study. Yet those discussions revealed that results had not always been immediately identifiable, nor readily traced to one source, nor indeed related to 'academic competence' (in the narrowest sense of the term), but they had arisen nevertheless; so although students had not always been immediately aware of changes occurring in their professional approach to problems in the workplace, those changes had nevertheless been real.

A feature of the current educational scene is the drive towards teaching to 'competencies'. My own view is that as a returning student you would be wise to treat talk of such things with a degree of caution. Competencies are attractive to those who organize and resource education because they offer the prospect of tangible results of training, things that can be aimed for and assessed in a fairly hard-nosed way. The danger is that all sorts of things get dressed up as competencies: for example, I have seen 'attitudes towards members of ethnic minorities' described as a competency, which can be confusing for those who are actually trying to learn and understand what they have learnt. If the notion of a competency as a product of learning has any meaning for you then it must be possible to imagine yourself engaging in a task (intellectual or practical) which would allow you to exhibit competency in a way which is recognizable by others at least, and is measurable at best. Just what anyone could do in this sense to enable them to exhibit a competent attitude to someone from an ethnic minority is hard to imagine. More importantly for you as a student, however, is the problem which arises when the *only* things that are valued in curriculum terms are those things that can be represented as competencies. In short, 'things to be learnt' may only become valued when learning objectives can readily be framed as competencies and learning outcomes easily identified and measured; my suggestion is that this is not to your advantage because there are necessarily things of value for you to learn which are not so readily reduced to competencies. You may wish to think through your own expectations of what will be 'valuable to learn' and set those valued outcomes against specific competencies.

Summary

In this chapter we have:

- considered your reasons for returning to study;
- examined your interpretations of learning and competence and contemplated how you can create the conditions most likely to produce effective learning during your course of studies;
- suggested that you need to see 'returning to study' as a process necessarily involving change to you as a learner.

Conclusion

You have chosen to return to study, and you need now to reconcile yourself to the implications of that choice. A useful text to keep in mind is the quotation from Domerque with which the chapter opened. You might choose to underpin your interpretation of your own return to study as an opportunity to improve your ability to think and learn rather than merely as a time to accumulate knowledge, skills or even simply good grades.

Brockbank and McGill (1998), while being directed at teachers rather than students, might be a useful book for you to read at this point because it offers insights into how teaching and learning can be a matter of facilitation rather than instruction. It will be helpful to see yourself as an active learner entering an environment in which you can learn, rather than as someone who has arrived to be instructed by others. Among the general study guides you might find it useful to refer to as you reorientate yourself to study are Beddows (1989) and Northedge (1990).

2

Thinking and learning

To be conscious that you are ignorant is a great step to knowledge.
(Benjamin Disraeli, *Sybil*, Book 1)

Overview

This chapter discusses the essentials of effective thinking and learning that underpin the approach taken throughout this book. It examines the place of critical thinking in the whole process of returning to study, and suggests that, by making your own learning a point of focus in your studying, you can improve your abilities as a learner as well as make the learning of particular material more efficient.

Introduction

As you read this chapter you will be reflecting on your own style as a learner and thinking about the need to engage with learning at an evaluative level, that is, to make value judgements about new knowledge and skills. The notion of reflection, acknowledged obliquely by Disraeli in the quotation above, is key to your progress as a thinker and a learner – the implication being that you need to think constructively about the limits of your knowledge and the boundaries of your professional skills.

The personal dimension to learning

Being conscious of ignorance

One of the things in my professional life which makes me uneasy is when a student returning to study on a professionally based course claims to know all that they need to know about their professional work and, by implication, not to need the course upon which they are about to embark. This is in part because I find it difficult to 'teach' someone with this initial belief about the value of study, but I am also aware of the difficulty for them as a learner. A sense of enquiry and an interest in the challenge of changing the way things are, and the way you are yourself, are an important part of any process of effective learning. The implication of Disraeli's words at the head of this chapter is that awareness that one does not know is prerequisite to coming to know about something. As a returning student you need to recognize that, despite previous learning and professional experience, there remain things which you can learn profitably about both your professional work and yourself as a learner. Introductory literature to courses for returning students within professional domains will tend to include motivational statements about the former kind of learning (that is, about the kinds of enhancement of professional knowledge and skill attainable within a given programme of study). The latter kind (learning about yourself as a learner), however, is often overlooked. Yet, as already noted, you need to conceive of your approaching course of study as an opportunity for self-improvement and self-fulfilment at a more fundamental level than the mere accumulation of more knowledge and skill.

To be successful at advanced study requires that you learn to monitor and evaluate your own patterns of thinking, learning and remembering. Of course, Disraeli's words only take us so far. Certainly it is important to be conscious that there are things about your professional work that you still need to learn, but it is also necessary to come to an understanding of how you have learnt what you have so far and how you are learning new material and new skills. In short, monitoring your progress as a learner is crucially important in becoming a more effective learner. Brockbank and McGill (1998) have some useful things to say about the central role of reflection in effective learning.

Recognition of possibilities, your own potential and your individual approach to learning

It may be some years since you undertook sustained study, and studying – often in addition to a heavy workload – may seem an unfamiliar and forbidding challenge. It is important, however, to recognize that you *can* make a successful return to study (the evidence is probably all around you) and that you already possess the kinds of skills that can be harnessed to enable you to work effectively. It may be a matter of taking a fresh look at the kinds of skills you use in your professional life that may be applicable to, or adaptable to, learning in the context of renewed academic study. You need to unravel for yourself the strategies that are most effective for you. At the risk of stating the obvious, learning is very much an individual business. All of us think and learn in different ways, some of which may seem superficial but many of which are fundamental. For example, the way in which individuals are able to use the visual representation of material in their learning will vary considerably. Diagrams, plans and illustrations will have different value across any range of students. One of the students (a therapist) who commented on some of the ideas in this book described the way in which she used a flow chart:

> To get a structure about a problem, to find my orientation, I use a flow chart. For example, when I prepare an exam or presentation I take key words and make it all fit on one side of A4. I make a path that has smaller paths leading off it. I use it with clients as well to give them another way of working.

Flow charts may not be something you find it easy to work with; this is simply an example of the kind of reflection you need to engage in – a topic which is pursued later in this chapter.

The need for critical thinking

You will already have got the message that study is about improving the mind as much as it is about learning particular things and gaining specific skills. What I want to argue for in this section is that there should be an inevitable symbiosis between your professional work and your return to study in terms of your developing critical thinking abilities. Professional work requires that you do more than react to events – necessarily it implies that you will be reflective and critical about what you do and the decisions that you make. It is also the case that advanced study requires you to think critically and to give evidence of that thought in the way you present your ideas, be it in oral or written form. Further, it is likely that if your programme of study focuses wholly or in part on professional issues (perhaps falling into the 'continuing professional development' category) then it will almost inevitably involve critical reflection on your professional practice. There is then a coming together of professional and academic work under the umbrella of 'critical thinking'. The intention of this section is to draw your attention to just some of the aspects of critical thinking in the hope that you will be able to make links for yourself between what is required in your professional work and what will be needed in your academic studies.

What counts as critical thinking

'Critical thinking' is a term which is widely used and abused in various parts of the literature. In this chapter it is used to describe a kind of thought processing which is more than routine and non-directed and which reaches levels of clarity and purposefulness that enable you to unravel problems which are within your range of knowledge and skills. The word 'range' is included here because it is important to recognize that critical thinking is, in one sense at least, independent of levels of knowledge and skill. You may operate in a mode of critical thought at your current level of knowledge and skill, whatever that may be. Of course, you may not reach a 'correct' conclusion in this sense, but that becomes less significant (in the academic setting if not in the real world of professional practice) than the fact that you are engaged in a critical way.

It might be helpful, therefore, if you can separate out your understanding of your ability to think from your knowing of things and your set of acquired practical skills. This is a rather artificial exercise and is not to say that knowledge and practical skills are unimportant, or less important than your ability to think, but simply to recognize that they need to take their place in the whole of your intellectual profile. It would be deceptive to conceive of your return to study as a matter of gaining in knowledge without recognizing the corresponding gain in thinking ability that is required.

Some students have reported that at the outset of their return to study they have a view of their intelligence as being fixed at a certain level. On further questioning, it has often become apparent that this view has been arrived at as a result of previous experiences of academic study. I have come to think that such a view is unhelpful in that it implies that study may bring about an increase in knowledge but that it will not change the supposedly immutable underlying ability to think. This is not the place for an extended discussion of the psychology of intelligence (on which topic entire libraries might be filled). However, if you have the view that intelligence is a fixed commodity that is carried around in the head and is relatively unchangeable, then this may lead you to miss the point of study and of the possibilities in it for you. The ability to reason and to think through problems clearly can be improved; intelligence, if you need to consider it at all, is best conceived of as a dynamic concerned with the ability to learn and to adapt as a result of learning. Rowntree (1988) might be an interesting book to consult on this subject.

Critical thinking in the professional context

The purpose of this subsection is to draw parallels between what you are likely to have experienced in your professional work and what you will need to consider in your academic studies. I have often sat in committee meetings trying to resolve apparently intractable problems (for example, how to develop a taught course to meet the needs of students from a wide range of disciplines while retaining the teaching of 'discipline-specific skills') and found myself wondering how and why this difficulty has come about. It is all too easy to find oneself locked into trying to find a solution and to lose sight of the reasons why the problem exists in the first place. Sometimes, in such meetings, people will wonder out loud what is the purpose of it all, which is often a reasonable question. The original purpose and definitions often need to be revisited and clarified in professional life, just as they do in an academic piece of work.

It is quite likely that you will be able to recall instances from your professional life where colleagues have reached conclusions without considering all of the relevant features of the situation (for example, interpreting a child's disturbed behaviour without considering all of the aspects of that child's home and school life), where justifications for decisions have failed to acknowledge all of the factors involved, where the implications of decisions were not thought through before implementation (for example, deciding on a planning application without considering its environmental consequences). All of these are instances of non-critical thinking, where people, however knowledgeable, have failed to use all of their critical faculties: they have thought too narrowly about the objective, they have used powers of rhetoric to make false justifications, or they have not thought beyond the immediate. In a similar way, there is a need to try to avoid these same pitfalls when you think through a problem set in the academic context and when you present your ideas to an academic audience.

To think critically means more than simply to be negative about something. Certainly, it involves finding fault. But critical thinking is a matter of finding fault with argument, with the basis upon which evidence is cited and with the reasonableness of conclusions reached. It is probably the case that in much of your professional life these things are implied. Colleagues may not set out their arguments, the bases for their acceptance of evidence and so on, for your convenience; all of these things may remain implicit. Critical thinking therefore requires a construction on your part of how things have come to be, as well as an analysis of what people say or do. When you have constructed in this way, for example, the history of a medical diagnosis that is under question then you can begin to analyse efficacy and begin to hypothesize about prognosis. The point of all this is to stress the link with academic work, where you are required to analyse what is written in the literature and what is claimed from empirical investigations using the accepted methodologies of your discipline. It may well be helpful if you conceive of critical thinking in the academic arena as an extension of what you already practice (perhaps unknowingly) in your professional life.

Task: Critical thinking in the professional context

Can you cite an example from your professional context which picks up on some aspect of non-critical thinking, for example:

- where individuals reach conclusions without considering all of the relevant features of the situation;
- where justifications for decisions reached fail to acknowledge all of the factors involved;
- where the implications of decisions are not thought through before implementation?

If so, try to write down where the process of critical thought has broken down – and, where possible, identify why that should have been so.

  Student responses

Non-critical thinking – when a professional doesn't see the need to have the background information about the client; for example, a client may have challenging behaviour and the professional tries to find a way of reducing this behaviour without finding its cause.

(Clinical psychologist)

When the government makes efforts to 'raise standards' in schools by, in part, increasing testing without realizing that continual assessment can be a distraction rather than an advantage for children's actual learning.

(Primary school teacher)

Analysing problem-solving protocols

A useful source of ideas on problem-solving protocols is the book by Halpern (1984). She goes into more detail than I have space for, but throughout her book the message is similar: you can improve your capabilities as a problem-solver through a process of analysis of your own problem-solving style and of the features inherent within the tasks that you face. The mechanical engineer facing a malfunctioning engine follows a problem-solving procedure, typically beginning with some hypotheses based on the kind of malfunction that is apparent. Similarly, that same engineer might set about tackling an academic assignment by following a problem-solving procedure, perhaps beginning by trying to make clear to him/herself just what the assignment brief requires and within what constraints the 'answer' is to be delivered – for example, whether it requires an illustration of an approach or the justification of a specific solution to a stated problem, and the maximum word count required. The difference between the professional and academic tasks is, of course, that the former may be more defined and practised than the latter. In any case, for you as a professional returning to study, analysing how you go about solving problems in either context is likely to be a profitable exercise; and profit in one domain is likely to feed into the other.

A defining feature of your profession or academic discipline might be that it requires you to follow certain general heuristics ('rule of thumb' procedures that are likely to set you in the direction of a correct response to the problem with which you are faced) or a specific algorithm (a procedure that will necessarily yield a correct solution if followed exactly). Professions and disciplines operate on particular ways of knowing and responding to problems. For example, a natural scientist may operate on an understanding of a set of fairly immutable laws of nature, whereas a social scientist may need to balance probabilities based on a critical understanding of the dynamics of social groups. It may help you to begin to unravel the way in which arguments and procedures are constructed in your area if you can set out a kind of protocol in which you 'think aloud' through a problem-solving process that is typical of your professional working routines.

Clearly, constructing this kind of problem-solving protocol might be a feature of your return to study in that you may find yourself having to make overt the process of problem-solving that you engage in regularly within your professional practice. In seminar discussions or in written assignments within the academic context you may have to analyse that process with a view, for example, to clarifying justifications you have made and identifying alternative possibilities. Similarly, it may help you to understand the way in which the academic arena operates if you think of, for example, a tutorial with your supervisor as a time when he/she is modelling for you the kinds of protocol that may be followed successfully in academic study. In this way study may be seen as just another problem-solving context in which certain rules pertain and certain protocols can be followed to your advantage.

Note, however, that there is a danger in breaking down a task into discrete identifiable stages and then treating these as if they have a reality beyond being descriptors of a process. It is often the synchrony between steps in a process that makes that process what it is. A solicitor who successfully carries through a divorce petition is doing more than going through a series of discrete steps. Breaking down a process into stages may be useful as a means of analysis, but we should remember that it is an artificial procedure which may lead to an artificial description and, if used as a way of training, may lead to an artificial kind of understanding. Consequently, an approach such as 'programmed learning', where learners proceed through sets of material packaged into small steps and delivered with an emphasis on repetition, can lead to a situation where those same learners lose sight of the overall meaning of the event, where the main ideas are obscured by the detail and where the way in which concepts are interrelated is not understood.

Taking account of context

One of the aspects of critical thinking that should be emphasized here, and which arises from the dangers of breaking down situations for analysis, is the need to consider the context as well as the problem. Academic study again mirrors professional work in requiring that you as a student consider a problem within the context in which it is set. An individual's views about a particular issue (such as the seriousness of the offence of driving without road tax) are likely to change if that issue is presented in different contexts (consider the offence of driving without road tax alongside dropping litter and driving across a road junction when the lights are on amber, and again alongside serial rape and armed robbery). In short, meaning can change according to context and in professional decision-making this phenomenon can create natural conflicts. Academic study which involves reflection on professional practice will therefore need to take this into account. It may well be the case that the non-critical response to a problem-solving scenario might be to offer clear-cut, universal solutions, whereas a critical response might be to offer an account in which context is accommodated as a variable with particular parameters of meaning.

Representation of problems

Table 2.1 sets out some of the different ways of representing whatever professional or academic problem faces you. These alternatives may provoke you to think about the way in which you first approach a problem-solving task.

Very often the first thing you have to do in problem-solving is to familiarize yourself with the problem state and its particular make-up. Thinking about how to represent problems should enable you to begin to think about how to manipulate elements of the problem in order to better understand it and so begin to find ways of resolving it. For example, it may be that you need to focus on just what it is that makes the problem difficult to resolve simply by asking: 'What *is* the problem exactly?' On the other hand, it may be that you need to unravel the overt and covert aspects of the problem: the paramedic faced with the 'brave' accident victim claiming to need low priority and who displays little visual evidence of injury needs to consider the possible effects of shock, the likelihood of internal injury in terms of the nature of the accident and so on. And again, if part of the difficulty of the problem you face is in its lack of definition then clarification may have to be your starting point. At a simple level, if you are not clear exactly what certain terms mean – for example, in an academic assignment title – then you may have to seek out meaning in, for example, a technical glossary. At a more complex level, it may be that lack of definition requires that you restate the goal in different forms – for example, achieving an 'appropriate placement' within social services provision

Table 2.1   Representing problems

Ways of representing	Examples of occasions for use	Possible advantages
Write down in words or figures	Where the presentation of the problem is oral.	Saves you the effort of trying to hold the problem state in your head.
Restate in your own words	Where the presentation is convoluted or deliberately opaque or ambiguous.	Helps you to see what you think you are trying to do – particularly useful in a group problem-solving context where different perceptions of the nature of the question may be helpful.
Draw a graph	Where the problem is spatial or involves relationships that change over time.	Can present all of the information at once; can simplify.
Draw a diagram	Where the problem relates to a process, or a set of relationships or the development of concepts.	Can show how a process fits together or relationships become operative.
Create a hierarchy or tree diagram	Where there are various possible outcomes or different, but equally feasible, routes to a solution.	Can help to unravel complex relationships; can indicate how one thing follows from another, etc.
Create a matrix	Where there are various combinations of results.	Can help to unravel the relationships between categories.

for an adult with learning difficulties might be interpreted as adapting her current environment rather than seeking out a new placement.

Strategies for solving problems

There is not space in this book to describe adequately all of the kinds of problem-solving strategies that might be available to you in the course of your studies. However, in this subsection we will look at a selection of approaches in order to give you an indication of the kinds of ideas that may improve the way in which you go about solving the variety of problems that you will encounter in your return to study.

A *means–ends analysis* will allow you to define sub-goals that, when achieved, should enable you to progress from the posing of a question to the main goal. It is a matter of analysing the problem that you face in terms of what means are required to get you to the desired outcome or end. It may be that in investigating, for example, how clients are treated at the first point of contact, you first need to look at the reasons for and circumstances behind that contact before you can make progress towards an understanding.

It may be possible, of course, to determine the means by working back from the end; that is, it may be that you can work backwards from the goal to your present questioning state. For example, if the problem relates to an unsatisfactory by-product in a particular process of food production then it may be necessary to work out how the by-product comes about before you can work out what can be done about the whole of the production process.

Brainstorming is the technique of setting down on paper as many ideas relating to a theme, or possible solutions to a problem, as you can in a random and spontaneous way. Some see this technique as merely a chance to say or write down anything that comes into the head without having to justify or explain it, while others see it as useful way to generate ideas without being restricted by artificial boundaries. Most commonly used as a group activity, there is no reason why it cannot be used on an individual basis. In my experience it carries with it the possible advantage of freeing students from the kinds of psychological constraints that sometimes impede problem-solving. If you feel locked into a particular kind of solution or 'accepted' way of proceeding, then letting your mind generate ideas in an unfettered way can be liberating. It is, however, likely to be only the first stage in a problem-solving process. Any list of ideas generated by brain-storming will still need to be refined, for example into categories and then into some kind of rank order of practicality, cost, acceptability and so on.

Using *analogy* in problem-solving is a matter of going through a process of reasoning by using parallel cases. You may have tried to explain something complex to a client who has no specialist knowledge and found yourself resorting to 'It's like . .' and then using an analogy which relates the technical to the everyday experience of that client – for example, 'when the water rises as you get into the bath' or 'the layers of an onion'. Just as analogy is useful in explaining complex material to others, so it can be a useful device in helping you to interpret a problem facing you. I have found with my students that encouraging them to develop an analogy for themselves allows them to recast a complex prob-lem which appears to be outside their range of experience into a form with which they are familiar so that they are then able to begin to manipulate ideas.

The three approaches noted above are discussed in more detail in Halpern (1984).

A place for originality and creativity

You might think that originality and creativity belong in the 'arts' disciplines and have little to do with other areas of academic study and professional life. This may be a misguided view. Often in higher education there will be open-ended tasks with outcomes which are not clearly defined in advance. What the task setter is looking for in such tasks is creativity and originality as much as accuracy, relevance and presentation. Similarly, the very nature of much professional work requires creative solutions to be found to everyday problems, and indeed some industrial companies reward workers for creative solutions to existing problems in the workplace.

In your academic study, as in your professional work, you are likely to need to think *divergently* as well as *convergently*; that is, to think around and beyond problems as well as to focus on a solution in the immediate. You are likely to need to express sensitivity to issues and to use imagination to predict outcomes. Also, I hope you will find that there is a place for risk-taking. Indeed, at the sharp edge of academic enquiry a project without any kind of intellectual risk attached is unlikely to prove profitable. Creativity may be hard to identify and to judge, but this does not deny its existence or lessen its value.

 Reflection: A place for creativity?

Is there a place for creativity in your professional work?

If there is, then:

• how is it manifest;
• how is it evaluated by you (if at all);
• how is it judged by others?

▶ **Student responses**

People think engineering is a matter of working systematically to achieve set goals, but in fact solving engineering problems is a very creative business ... I guess our creativity is not really evaluated as such − but the results are.

(Engineer)

The highest praise my partner has heaped upon me is to say that I have completed some of the most imaginative bridgework he has ever seen.

(Dental surgeon)

If you are particularly interested in trying to become more creative in your approach to problem-solving then you may find some useful ideas and strategies in Parnes *et al.* (1977).

Reflection

Reflection as a way to effective learning

Having a range of problem-solving techniques and creative strategies at your fingertips will undoubtedly help you to learn. An equally important element in the learning process, however, is the capacity for reflection. I know that all the students I meet who are re-entering the world of study *can* learn, but I am also aware that those who will become the more effective learners are those who find ways of reflecting on their own learning and therefore give themselves opportunities to take control over that learning.

Evaluative appraisal

The defining feature of reflection, which distinguishes it from mere recall, is that it contains some evaluation of what has happened. A necessary feature of effective learning is that it involves an ongoing process of evaluating what is being learnt in terms of its effect on one's wider knowledge and ability to understand issues – failure to engage with learning in this evaluative way is likely to lead to a restricted understanding. You may doubt this and cite examples from your own experience where learning by rote – without any evaluative appraisal – has been effective for you. But if you think carefully about the effects of such rote learning then you may recognize that while you can learn information by rote, that learning is likely to be limited: firstly, there are limits to how much you can learn in this way; and secondly, recall of that information is constrained by the need for the appropriate cues. As a student in higher education you need to be able to think flexibly and in a self-initiated way, and you cannot afford to be dependent on any particular set of cues.

As a student, therefore, it will be helpful to find ways in which you can operate at a judgemental level with regard to material to be learnt and the way in which it is presented. You might try to engage with new learning at a personal level, asking yourself how it affects *you* and the way *you* understand the world. Notions that learning and problem-solving require objectivity are misleading. It is subjectivity that denotes learning as being of the human kind and that takes it out of the realms of what, for example, a computer can 'learn'. It would be inappropriate here to be side-tracked into a discussion of artificial intelligence, but a cursory glance at the literature will indicate that teaching computers to perform tasks is one thing but teaching them to *think* (in the real sense of the term) is another. If you can engage with learning at a level that involves you in personal evaluative appraisal of both what is being learnt and the way you are learning it, you may both learn particular material in a more meaningful way and make yourself a more effective learner in the long term. Brockbank and McGill (1998) explore the significance of emotion and action in learning. They also emphasize the need for lecturers to engage in dialogue with students: and it is the need for dialogue to which we now turn.

Making use of an 'active listener'

It may well be that, in your return to study, there is an important role to be played by someone operating as an 'active listener' – that is, listening and reflecting back to you what you appear to be saying so that greater clarity can be achieved. Students working in isolation sometimes have difficulty in developing their ideas if they do not have some way of making their views known to another and getting constructive feedback. Of course, this kind of dialogue can be achieved in the process of handing in assignments and receiving back comments, but that process inevitably involves delay and does not always allow a debate of the kind which is envisaged here. Somehow you need to try to make use of someone who can listen to what you say and engage with you in a discussion about it. Certainly, some of the students who commented on the ideas in this book found some use for this notion:

> Yes it is very important to have it to get another perspective on a subject that may open up other alternatives that you may not have thought of . . . you can then pursue these ideas if desired.
>
> (Engineer)

I am totally reliant on a person who acts as what you call a 'critical friend'. Without talking to her I don't think I'd know what I think about anything at all – I need her there to bounce ideas off.

(Environmental scientist)

I think someone once said something about not knowing what he thought until he heard what he said – well, for me there is some truth in that and certainly it goes one step further if someone else can tell me what they think I am getting at. I use people at work – one bloke in particular who seems good at saying things like 'so you mean that . . .'.

(Industrial chemist)

Summary

- The ideas which underpin this book have been introduced and the benefits of an active and evaluative approach have been highlighted.
- It is important to begin to think of strategies for adopting a critical, reflective approach in your studies. These strategies may or may not involve others and will operate at different levels of formality. As with much of returning to study, the choice is necessarily and properly yours.

Conclusion

If, in a self-evaluative sense, you can say that you have recognized things in the world that you do not fully understand and recognized things about yourself as a learner, then you can reassure yourself that you have taken the step, recommended by Disraeli in the quotation at the beginning of this chapter, towards knowledge both of things and of yourself. Alongside this self-awareness needs to be a determination to develop critical faculties as well as to accumulate knowledge. As Confucius (551–479 BC) noted: 'Learning without thought is labour lost; thought without learning is perilous'.

3

Working and communicating with others

I do then with my friends as I do with my books. I would have them where I can find them, but I seldom use them.

(Ralph Waldo Emerson)

Overview

In this chapter you will:

- examine ways of working effectively with peers and tutors;
- consider ways of becoming aware of your existing levels of personal knowledge, ways of increasing that knowledge base and extending your personal skills and ways of relating to peer and group assessment;
- look at ways of improving your ability to communicate ideas and information in oral presentations.

Introduction

Most study is organized in social contexts (even distance learning courses tend to have points of contact between tutors and students and between students and their peers). Yet the possibilities of learning *through* the social aspects of the setting, as well as simply learning *within* it, are not always fully explored. If we widen the interpretation of 'friends' in the above quotation from Emerson to include colleagues, peers and tutors, then many students in my experience have treated their 'friends' in much the same way as Emerson did: they are there but they are not used. While it may seem somewhat calculating and manipulative to suggest that you conceive of your friends and colleagues as useful material for your own progression as a student, I would argue that learning can be enhanced by those around you. In this chapter I try to unravel the social dimension to learning for you as a returning student from the professions.

Working effectively in groups

Group learning contexts

In the introduction to this chapter I suggest that learning in a social context is a process with opportunities that you might wish to exploit to the full. There is another, perhaps less laudable but still pertinent factor which needs consideration, namely that you may find 'learning in groups' to be a necessary aspect of your return to study. You may have no choice but to engage with learning in this way.

We need, at this point, to draw a distinction between working *in* a group and working *as* a group. In the former case you are assigned with other students to a group (with or without some credible rationale for its composition) and expected to learn some set of information or array of skills that is predetermined by your tutor and presented to you as an individual group member. In the latter case you are expected to collaborate with others in the resolution of problems (not necessarily predetermined), and the learning is concerned with how you operate as a group member. Working in a group requires little discussion here; certainly there will be issues of sharing resources and determining goals, but as a professional you will most likely have encountered these kinds of working conditions consistently in your everyday practice. Working as a group, however, needs a little further exploration.

Peer assessment

Your profession may validate its own procedures by a process of peer assessment. Academia itself is steeped in the notion that peer assessment is an appropriate way of validating new courses and approving grades awarded on existing ones. If your particular programme of study incorporates some element of peer assessment then you should examine carefully how the assessment criteria are defined and how they are described to you and your fellow assessors. There are potential gains for you as a learner in a well-organized scheme of peer assessment, which can be summarized as follows:

- As an assessor of other students you will have access to the criteria by which judgements are made and how they are operated in practice. (Clearly knowing the criteria against which judgements of standard are being made enables you to have clear targets as to what you need to produce in order to achieve good grades.)
- As both a recipient of such assessment and an assessor, you are likely to become aware of how different perceptions of your work can exist and yet be resolved in coming to an agreed judgement.

However, there are also potential hazards: you might find that the process of peer assessment proves divisive within your group of peers, and if the issue of common understanding of expected standards is unresolved then judgements made will relate to some other set of criteria which are both unofficial and perhaps untenable. For example, peers might give value to the perceived amount of effort that has gone into something – this may or may not be a legitimate factor to take into account.

Group-based assessment

It may be that your course incorporates some elements of group-based assessment. If so, then tasks are likely to be set which require group interaction and which are therefore amenable to assessment either of the product of your group's effort or of the process of your group's interaction. For example, your group might be assessed on its collective production of solutions to a given problem (for example, that of moving group members and equipment across an obstacle course or the planning of a new leisure complex on a greenfield site with minimum environmental cost). Alternatively, it may be that individuals are assessed on their participation within your group (on their contribution to the successful solution to the obstacle course problem or on their role in the designing of the leisure complex). Clearly, it is important to make yourself aware of the particular parameters of specific tasks and their assessment. You will find it helpful in knowing how to direct your energies if you can find out from course documentation, or direct from tutors, what the purpose of this form of assessment is and what the perceived advantages are for you (as opposed to advantages for course organizers). The response you get is likely to be that the perceived gains are those of developing group cohesion and a sense of shared responsibility, as well as of increasing awareness of individual roles within groups and of the processes which underpin the making of judgements. This can all be seen as having significant potential benefits for your development as a learner.

Roles and responsibilities of group members

Any group operates on the basis that its members take on certain roles and responsibilities – for example, as leader, critic, scribe or arbitrator. Some group members seem to create tension and some will attempt to defuse it, perhaps by seeking compromise or conciliation. Different situations often require different kinds of role to be fulfilled, and a group will develop over time with roles shifting as the demands of the particular task change or as new aspects of the situation are revealed. It is also the case that individuals are not always aware of the roles they tend to play in group situations. This is certainly to oversimplify what is a very complex business, but the important point is that you need, as a learner in a group context, to form some understanding of how your particular group is operating. By your very membership of the group you will become part of the dynamic that operates within it, even if you withdraw from the direction that it takes.

Being in the artificial situation of a learning group in a university can become a useful opportunity for you to explore the kinds of currents and pressures that pertain in groups. This will enable you to come to a clearer understanding of how groups operate in your normal professional background and, in particular, how you operate within those groups. Group learning activities give you the chance to find out about how and why you lead or you follow, how you go about asserting yourself and your views, how readily you succumb to the views of others and to group pressure for consensus, how successful you can be at accommodating the views of others, at achieving consensus among disparate viewpoints, at negotiating to resolve tensions.

Forming and maintaining a study syndicate

You may be able to form a study syndicate with other students on your course (or join an existing one). Broadly speaking, in such a syndicate resources and books are shared, ideas are discussed, physical help is given with the design and implementation of experimental work, feedback is given on drafts of submissions or on initial results of experimental work and so on. This can certainly be very beneficial. However, it is worth noting that study syndicates tend to operate less effectively in direct relation to the amount of competition that arises within the process of assessment (clearly competition for grades among group members is unlikely to foster collegiality). Despite this warning note, if clear understandings between all members of the syndicate are established at the outset then significant gains are possible for each member in both amount of work achieved and social interchange. In my experience, syndicates have worked best when they have been self-generating and self-sustaining; attempts by staff to impose such syndicates have foundered where members have not been able to establish and maintain a true cooperative spirit.

Accessing knowledge

In this section we will look at ways in which you can gain access to knowledge above and beyond the obvious library routes which are discussed in later chapters. At this point the concern is with communication as much as sources of information.

Professional associations

One feature of your return to study that may distinguish it from that of the non-professional is the existence of a professional association in your field. Professional organizations may act as repositories of knowledge and in some cases as gatekeepers for the development of knowledge in the sense that they may act to validate developments and may control to a greater or lesser extent the process of dissemination. For example, your professional organization may have sections which publish professional journals containing refereed articles (the process of refereeing is one of validation by peer review) and thus that organization acts as a conduit for the ideas and practical developments within that professional discipline. As a side issue I cannot resist noting that if Nietzsche was right when he wrote about knowledge working as a tool of power and increasing with every increase of power (Nietzsche, 1968) then it may be assumed that a professional body that 'controls' knowledge increases its own viability, power and independence within the wider social scene.

The extent to which this matters to your academic study depends on the strength of the links between academia and your particular profession (for example, can you practise only when you have certain academically validated qualifications?) and on whether the focus of your programme of study is on professional development itself or on the development of intellectual abilities of a more general kind (as in the distinction between the 'professional' and the 'traditional' doctorate). But whatever the case, it will be useful to think through the way in which you can use your professional organization to help you to gain access to knowledge.

Information technology

There will almost inevitably have been advances in the speed and flexibility in communications since your last experience of study. Thus it is important to your successful return to study that you find out about the availability of new ways of accessing information. *The internet* often makes information accessible long before it is available in bookshops and libraries. Increasingly, for example, official reports and the results of findings from authorized investigations are posted on the internet at the same time as they are released to the press and into bookshops. Getting information from the internet and using it in your own writing can cause problems in terms of referencing your sources (material presented *only* in electronic form may be hard to claim as a source which is readily and permanently accessible within the public domain, which is the claim you can and do make when you reference or quote a source 'in the literature'). However, becoming knowledgeable requires that you make full use of all avenues for finding out the latest information and views – and the internet is likely to be key in this respect. Indeed, it is not solely a matter of what material you can access from what is on the internet, but also what you can share and what you can proactively find through the internet. For example, you may want to consider creating your own web page if you are developing an interest in a particular area. Again, you would need to refer to a specialist text for information as to how to proceed, but the difficulties might not be as daunting as you may think and the possibilities rewarding. Two books that you may find useful are Hardie and Neou (1994) and Harmon (1996).

Electronic mailing lists offer an informal and fast way of exchanging information and ideas. Your profession may well have some form of both official and unofficial such lists. The latter sometimes perform a subversive function by giving wide access to individuals or subgroups with idiosyncratic, or at least non-legitimized, agendas. In direct contrast to the professional 'voice' provided by authorized, peer-reviewed journals and papers, informal mailing lists and noticeboards provide an outlet for opinion and non-validated findings and procedures. As a returning student, both may be important to you. Official sources give you the kind of 'validated' information that you need to refer to in your writing, whereas informal mailing lists can give you an insight into a range of views and different kinds of professional developments that are ongoing. The trick, of course, is to learn to distinguish between what is worthwhile and what is not.

Colleagues in the workplace

Discussions with students have suggested that their return to study has often resulted in changes to the way in which they have related to others in their professional context. Certainly, if the course of study on which you embark is professionally orientated then it should provoke you to question the way in which things are done and to investigate the potential of different procedures and so on. Indeed, if it does not provoke you in these ways then you may need to ask yourself if there is something in you, or in the course itself, that is getting in the way of what should be a natural product of such study.

Developing your working relationships in such a way as to make the most of your colleagues' knowledge and experience will clearly help you to 'become knowledgeable'. It will have benefits for your studies, but there is also likely to be an expectation on the part of colleagues that you will be prepared to share with them some of the ideas and information gained from your studies. Establishing networks of professional colleagues with whom you can discuss issues may well be a significant aspect of the whole business of successful study and professional enhancement. Many colleagues will treat investigatory questions from you as interesting and valuable, especially if you are sensitive in the phrasing of such questions and mindful of the work pressures on others.

Oral presentations

Oral presentations in the professional context

One of the more clearly defined and significant aspects of working and communicating with others is the giving of oral presentations. But before discussing some of the detail of giving such presentations, it is worth making another link between what you do in your professional work and what formal study may demand of you. Your professional work may well involve some kind of interface with colleagues where you are required to convey your views, findings or conclusions, and increasingly the interface may extend to other professional and non-professional areas. You may therefore already have experience of public speaking in one form or another, and it may be a matter of drawing on that experience and adapting what you have learnt to the academic setting.

You may have experienced different kinds of pressure when speaking to those from within your own intellectual discipline and professional background than when speaking to a lay audience. This is not to suggest that either one is inherently more difficult than the other, but that accepted knowledge of technical language and level of ability and understanding as well as perspective on, and likely attitude towards, issues will necessarily affect the way in which you approach the task of presenting ideas. What you need to do here is to reflect upon why there should be a difference between what is required of you by different audiences and what you have learnt about your own difficulties and potentials in talking to groups of people.

Structuring academic oral presentations

An academic oral presentation needs organizing in much the same way as does a written piece of work. You need to clarify for yourself what the main points are that you wish to convey, how you will introduce your topic and how you will draw it to a conclusion. Then you need to put yourself in the position of your listeners and decide how what is already clear to you can become clear to them. You may need to present the overall structure of the talk for them at the outset, and then proceed to fill in the detail. You might do this verbally, or more likely you will use some kind of visual representation (such as an outline in bullet points shown on an overhead projector). A visual representation serves to remind your listeners (and yourself!) where you have got to in the overall plan. Clearly the need for this kind of structuring increases with the complexity of the information to be presented.

Using notes during an oral presentation

One issue that needs resolving early on is the degree of formality of the talk (for example, whether there will be an ongoing dialogue with the audience or not) and the possibility and appropriateness of using notes. The more you rely on the reading of notes, the less natural your presentation may seem. Of course, there are occasions where literally 'reading a paper' is the appropriate format (and there are some discipline areas where such reading is commonplace if not obligatory). The judgement must be yours, but it is an important one which has significant implications for the way in which your presentation is likely to be received. Most of us would probably agree that it is more difficult to engage with the ideas a speaker is trying to get across when he/she is reading from a script rather than speaking naturally. Equally, however, listening to someone who is talking in an unfocused and unstructured way within an academic context can be frustrating. A useful compromise which many colleagues use is to have a written talk which is then reduced to a series of points. These points can be written on cards and used as prompts. This approach enables you to adhere to some kind of academic rigour and at the same time retain the naturalness that aids accessibility for your audience.

Practising oral presentations

Some people find it helpful to rehearse what they are to say in the actual room that is to be used, and certainly even experienced academic speakers will often want to inspect the venue and to check out the facilities and the physical nature of the space (speaker system, visual displays, podium, acoustics and so on) before they stand up to speak. I have heard it suggested that it is easier to remember what you need to say if you practise in the actual room that is to be used. Whether this is true or not, practice does give you the chance to translate the structure you have decided upon into the practicalities of giving the presentation. For example, if you are using an overhead projector then it is helpful to know which side of it you will stand, where you will stack your acetates or slides and where you will put them when you have finished with them. This kind of knowledge enables your presentation to go more smoothly and avoids distracting the audience.

Of course, it may not be possible to practise your presentation in the actual venue, but the benefits of rehearsal remain. A practice enables you to: work out what you are to say at each stage of the talk (in relation to each acetate or slide if you are using such), make sure that the sequencing of ideas or major points is appropriate, and confirm that your estimations of timing are reasonably accurate. On this last point of timing, rehearsing a presentation silently 'in your head' is unlikely to give you an accurate indication of timing – you will tend to take longer when you come to actually speak the words. It is difficult to judge the time it will take to deliver a given amount of material, so it is a good idea to be flexible in what you expect to cover in the time permitted. For example, you might include sections in your prepared material that can be cut, without losing the sense of the whole, if you judge as you talk that time is running short; or it might be possible for you to plan for a number of alternative end points, so that you can stop at a convenient one when your allotted time runs out. Of course, your audience does not need to know that sections have been cut or that there are different endings – hopefully what they see and hear will be an apparently complete performance which comes to an end naturally at a predetermined time.

Observing other speakers

Just as it is important to look at other people's writing that you value and try to learn how they get across their ideas, structure their work, and phrase their sentences, so it can be very profitable for you to pay attention to how someone you perceive to be a good speaker works at his/her task. A successful academic oral presentation does not happen by magic; though it may seem effortless it will inevitably be the result of experience, learned skills and careful thought and preparation. You need to observe not just *what* is being said by the good speaker but also *how* it is being said – asking yourself how it is that the speaker is so convincing and understandable, how he/she employs strategies to clarify ideas, gain and hold the attention of the audience and so on. Watching a consummate performer is an opportunity for you to learn about the art of performance as well as about the particular content concerned.

Task: Learning from a good example

Recall an example of a presenter who impressed you as a good speaker or, better still, an instance of a talk that you thought to be good. Note down features of the speaker or the talk which you think contributed to its quality. Can you adapt any of these features for use in your own oral presentations?

▶ **Student responses**

The features of the good talk were: confidence, eye contact, presence, elaborating (off the cuff) from single points. I think the lecturer had prepared thoroughly − I need to adapt her 'knowing the subject confidently and not giving it in too much detail'. Above all, I need to practice.

(Information scientist)

I think it was pace really. She kept my attention by somehow varying the speed at which she talked. It was something to do with the way she led up to a point then summarized it for me then started again and slowly built up to the next one. That and the fact that she was funny − without seeming to tell jokes she made me laugh − I think it was the way she said what she said rather than what she said in itself.

(Environmental scientist)

Recognizing the constraints on your oral presentation

A significant aspect of planning and practice is recognition of the limitations of the talk you are to give. In particular, you will be limited by time and by the capabilities of your audience (this is not to denigrate your likely audience but to stress that no audience can cope with too many ideas or facts presented in too short a time). These two limitations combine to create perhaps the most significant aspect of your advance organization and rehearsal: the need to cover a limited number of key ideas or components of information in the specified time without undue haste. In a 20-minute talk you should reckon to cover only one or two main ideas or themes, and there is a case for keeping *any* presentation to a maximum of 50 minutes. Certainly, the ability of an audience to listen and actively attend to detail will diminish as time goes on and more ideas are presented. It will help to recognize this and, where a long talk is required, respond by:

- alerting the audience to the structure of the talk before you begin;
- dividing up your 'text' into sections that enable the audience to accommodate new ideas systematically;
- presenting ideas thematically with reminders of what you have just covered and signposts to indicate where you are leading your listeners;
- breaking up your talk with activities for the audience or opportunities for them to discuss points with others;
- returning full circle to the main issues at the end of the presentation by way of summary.

Using overhead transparencies and slides

Academic presentations are very often accompanied by overhead transparencies (sometimes referred to as acetates) or slides because they offer the speaker visual props for his/her spoken words. They give the audience something to focus on as well as the spoken word. They can be used as an *aide-mémoire* in much the same way as the cards mentioned earlier. It is hard to overstate the importance of a good set of transparencies as the basis for a successful talk, and a great deal of time and effort should go into their preparation. You need to develop your use of transparencies to suit your own style of delivering an oral presentation, but some general guidance might be offered as follows:

- Slides should be kept simple, with as few words used as possible.
- Always use a big bold typeface, and make sure that your words are readable from the back of the room.

- Use diagrammatic information where it can usefully summarize and therefore replace text.
- Use bullet points or their equivalent.
- An overview of the whole talk at the outset on one slide is helpful in setting the scene and enabling the listeners to organize their attention in advance of your spoken words.
- Avoid standing in front of the screen as you speak.
- Avoid speaking 'to' the screen with your back to the audience.

You may find the articles by Allison and Bramwell (1994) and Norris (1978) useful. Don't be put off by their biological orientation: the points they make are quite generalizable to other disciplines.

Relationships with tutors or supervisors

Student–tutor relationships

During my experience of working with returning students from the professions there have been aspects of the teacher–student relationship in the professional context that I think I as a lecturer have needed to come to terms with and I think it is also the case that my students have needed to recognize that their professional status requires of them certain understandings. I think it is helpful then if you consider your own place in terms of the kinds of relationships that are likely to exist between you as a professional and your academic tutors. For example, there may be serious and complex ethical issues which need to be taken into account when you embark on any kind of practical investigation in your professional workplace. These may relate to matters of confidentiality relating to clients or to issues of possible 'abuse of power' if your studying requires that you analyse and discuss in seminars, or in written submissions, working relationships and practices that involve those working for you in a supporting role. Again, a hallmark of many professions is that care and concern for clients is paramount; if there is any possibility that your engaging in study may be to the detriment of your clients (perhaps because you are focusing on your own need to reflect on professional practice rather than their needs as clients) then clearly you may be in conflict with your own professional standards and etiquette. Usually, of course, there is no conflict and successful studying and professional work of benefit to the client group are synonymous. The issue of ethics is revisited in Chapter 7.

There is another aspect of the relationship between you and potential tutors that is worth mentioning: that of contrasting levels of experience. Your academic tutors may not have as much recent and relevant experience as you (although in many professional contexts such experience is a continuing requirement of academics) but that may not be as important as the skills of, for example, observation and analysis that they bring to the situation. They may not need experience of the kind that you have to do their job effectively if their job is defined in terms of, for example, observation and analysis. It is not so much a matter of your needing to respect the academic tutor regardless of his/ her lack of experience as, perhaps, of recognizing what skills and knowledge they *do* bring to the situation so that you can find ways of accessing those skills and knowledge for your own benefit.

Codes of Practice and Notes of Guidance

On the assumption that you intend to get the most out of the course of study on which you embark, it is worth ending this chapter by mentioning the expectations you are entitled to hold of the institution in which you study, and similarly the expectations it will hold of you. Commonly practices will be defined within a higher education institution which are accepted as minimum requirements or guidelines as to the way in which tutors and students should operate. Codes of Practice and Notes of Guidance should give you some idea of what you can expect in terms of, for example, time allocated for tutorials, resources and nature and extent of feedback. While such documents may seem of low priority in the early stages of registration and acclimatization to academia, it may help you get the most out of the institution if you read through them before you become embroiled in the various aspects of study. Establishing mutual expectations is a matter of importance: you need to know what is expected of you so that (assuming it is reasonable) you can do your best to deliver, and you need to know what you can expect of the institution so that you can make the best use of what is available.

Summary

In this chapter you have had the opportunity to consider:

- how you might approach issues of working effectively in the kinds of group situations that operate in your professional setting and the kinds of group learning situations that you are likely to encounter in your return to study;
- ways of increasing your awareness of your own knowledge and possibilities for increasing it and enhancing your range personal skills as well as your understanding of peer and group assessment;
- how you might improve your communication during oral presentations;
- how you can make the most of working relationships with other students and academic staff.

Conclusion

How similar are you to Ralph Emerson in your treatment of friends and colleagues: do you like to know that they are there but seldom if ever make the most of them? The first theme of this chapter has been that, as a professional, you need to recognize how your professional work brings you into contact with groups and individuals, professional or otherwise, and what you need to do to make yourself a more effective social operator in these contexts. The first step towards improvement may be to recognize realities and possibilities: what goes on in these respects in your professional life and what can you do about it (assuming something needs to be done). The second theme has been that working with others is likely to be an integral part of your return to study, and that it may be helpful to interpret group learning situations in academia as useful opportunities to enhance your own performance as a learner as well as to learn specific content effectively.

4

Effective reading and listening

The greatest part of a writer's time is spent in reading, in order to write; a man will turn over half a library to make one book.

(Samuel Johnson, from James Boswell, *The Life of Johnson*)

Overview

This chapter deals with accessing information and ideas, be it from books or from speakers. We will consider:

- how to choose what to read as well as how you can make the process of reading more efficient in terms of your own learning;
- different kinds of information sources and their relative usefulness in your studies;
- ways of using your note-taking as an effective learning strategy;
- the importance of developing a bank of references and a system for dealing with ideas as they arise.

Introduction

Samuel Johnson may not have had higher education students in mind when he talked of the 'greatest part of a writer's time'.

But the notion that to produce worthwhile text requires input in the form of reading holds true in today's academic world just as it did in the eighteenth century. As a professional returning to study you may think that you know enough to write an essay without worrying too much about the troublesome business of reading, but experience will soon teach you otherwise. We speak of students 'reading' for a degree, and with good reason.

In your own course of study you may not have the opportunity to listen to lectures and seminars, though it is likely that you will at least have the opportunity to listen to someone talking about academic matters in tutorial settings. Wherever the opportunity exists, it needs to be exploited. And while listening may seem an everyday thing that you apparently do automatically, it requires skill if it is to be utilized effectively in the context of learning at university level.

To complement your reading of this chapter you might like to refer to Fairbairn and Winch (1996).

Effective reading

Reading lists and key journals

If you are doing a taught course then it is most likely that you will be provided with lists of introductory or core reading. Such reading lists typically aim to encompass basic concepts and ideas, often with suggestions for further reading to clarify particular issues. They also often provide references for particular taught sessions or topics. Academics vary in their views on how essential core readings are likely to be. A more open-minded tutor may well encourage students to read books and articles that are not on the recommended lists for particular courses. Indeed, it could be argued that essential reading lists can be counter-productive to true intellectual enquiry because they necessarily limit the range of reading of the student and lead to a single accepted view (this would diminish the likelihood of achieving the kind of creativity discussed in Chapter 2). Certainly, there can be something of a self-perpetuating spiral of increasing narrowness and dependency where students seek out the text(s) which expound the views accepted by the assessor of their work and where tutors feed students only with titles with which they are familiar and which are therefore unlikely to provoke new and challenging intellectual debate.

If you are returning to study at a higher level than ever before, then it is important to note that while reading from set texts and regurgitating specific information in an acceptable form may sometimes be seen as desirable, this is not necessarily so at all levels. You need to be careful here and make judgements which relate to particular tutors and to specific discipline areas. These judgements need to be made in the context of a recognition that although a tutor may have recommended certain books there may well be other books, adjacent on the shelves to those recommended, that are equally useful. No book has a monopoly on truth and you should remain critically aware of the range of literature, whether the book or article is recommended or not.

Clearly, if you are registered for a degree within a specialist domain you will need to become aware of the journals in your particular area and of their relative importance. The above point about monopoly on truth applies here as well, though it may be extended to embrace schools of thought. There is an ever present danger when working within one particular academic sphere of influence that it may have an in-built resistance to ideas from outside and that therefore contrary ideas and perspectives are ignored.

Volume of material

One argument that is used to justify prescriptive reading lists is that students need to be helped through the large amounts of written material that exist on any given topic. Certainly, the amount of material you need to read in order to come to an understanding of any particular subject area may seem daunting when you first return to study, though of course you may have become accustomed to reading copious amounts of documentation in your professional work. What is important, of course, is that you try to make judgements about the quality of the different readings that are recommended to you.

Clearly the quantity and the level of difficulty of reading you have to cover, will vary according to your subject area: in relatively new areas little may have been published, yet in more established areas the opposite is likely to be true. If little has been published in your area then you will need to search widely for it. Conversely, if you are working in an established, well-documented area then you would be advised to try to identify significant parts of the literature and focus upon those in a way which is relevant to the particular project or assignment that you have in hand.

 Reflection: Your area of study

Is your chosen area of study relatively new or has it been established over a period of time? What are the implications of this for you?

 Student responses

This area has been around for about 40 years; however, it is only recent technological advances that have made implementation possible.

(Medical engineer)

Relatively old, still loads written on it, no real implementations – all research builds on what's gone on before, whether 'new' or established. All existing knowledge is open to challenge which makes it difficult sometimes for me as a student to draw conclusions.

(Nurse)

Almost completely new in specific terms, there is no 'one' journal from which to get relevant information, it is difficult to tease out pieces which are salient.

(Government lawyer)

Narrowing down your reading

I have already talked about the need to focus. In the first instance
at least, it would be a good idea to focus on the small number of
papers or books that are 'seminal' to your chosen area. This means
those books which are widely accepted as the most influential. It
may seem a little difficult to determine, in the early days of your
studies, exactly which those are. This is where academic tutors
should be able to help, but in seeking such guidance you need to
be clear about what you want to know. You should not expect
you tutor to do your thinking, nor indeed your searching, for
you; rather you should be asking to be pointed in the right direction. To ask for guidance effectively therefore, you need to have
thought about the purpose behind your reading.

Your academic area may have documents devoted entirely to
abstracts of articles or copies of contents pages of journals or
publications which give an index of works in particular areas.
Simply browsing through these can give you an idea of which
authors crop up most frequently and therefore which texts are
likely to be viewed as seminal. Note, however, that an author's
'popularity' is no indicator of universal merit in his/her work; it
is up to you to try to decide what is useful for you in terms of
the particular academic issues you need to address. You need to
make judgements about the relative merit of different texts and
what reading is likely to inform your understanding of a particular question. It may also be possible to determine by this kind of
searching which are the key issues and concerns of the moment
(remembering that in the academic world just as in the professional the perceived importance of issues changes over time,
emphases shift and new problems arise). Particularly useful are
editions of journals in which there are articles followed by secondary articles which respond to points made in them. Public
arguments of this kind are good for academics because they generate further debate (and thus further publications), but they are
also good for you as a student in that contrasting views are set
out for you (thus completing some of your groundwork).

If you are engaging in study for a higher award or degree with
a significant element of personal research then you may need to
spend a considerable amount of time and energy finding out about
the parameters as well as the detail of literature in your area.

Clearly, if you are engaged in study which is intended to enable you to push back the 'boundaries of knowledge' then, as a prerequisite, you need to know where those boundaries are. If you are working on an interdisciplinary project the task is more complex, and it may be crucial to the ultimate success of your project that you make appropriate links and define carefully the parameters of your literature searches. If your personal research is within education or the social sciences then you might find it helpful to refer to Denscombe (1998), which deals with the methods needed for specific pieces of small-scale research; or Bell (1993), which is particularly clear and helpful for first-time researchers.

Making use of journals

Whatever academic area(s) you work within will be populated by journals of varying quality and importance which can be rated according to different criteria. For example, there are 'league tables' which rank journals according to the number of times articles within them are cited by other journals. This self-reinforcing procedure gives you one kind of information, but in many areas there are journals which are rarely cited but none the less significant. In academic areas which are closely related to particular professions there are often journals which dominate in terms of disseminating new information and new findings. There are also what are often termed 'professional journals' which may lack academic kudos but nevertheless are influential in setting or reflecting trends of thought. As a returning student it is vital to become familiar with what is published where within your chosen area and to begin to make judgements about the purpose of journals and therefore their usefulness for your own cause.

As noted above, there are gradations of journals in most areas, sometimes ill defined but none the less pertinent. It is likely that for your purposes the better journals will be those where articles only appear after a process known as 'refereeing'. Refereed journals contain only articles that have passed some kind of test in terms of being well founded in reasonable research and scholarship. The testing is done by a process of peer review which acts in a limited way to validate the work as being of a certain standard. These kinds of journal are a particularly useful source of information for you when studying at advanced level because of their inherent sense of validity, derived from the fact that they have been, in some sense, tested out by experts in the field. It is important to note, though, that you do retain the right to challenge them!

Reading academic texts

Any kind of reading is a skill that takes practice to learn, and reading for the purposes of advanced study is no exception. To get a feel for what a piece of text is about, you may find it helpful to develop your ability to scan rather than read it in the first instance – again, you may already have this ability because of the peculiar pressures of your professional work. Most articles in academic journals have abstracts which essentially do some of this work for you by summarizing content; if you are lucky, therefore, you may find that all you need to scan is an abstract. Clearly, if your initial scanning indicates that further reading is likely to yield results then your next step would be to search for the part of the text that has the material of interest. It is not necessary at this stage to start reading all of the text from the beginning; indeed, you may find that looking at the concluding discussion is a useful way to start or that looking through the references or the bibliography at the outset gives a flavour for the kind of issues that are to be covered. Obviously you might decide to go back and read the whole text through but you need to be careful, because of the likely pressures of time, that you do this only if it seems worthwhile. Remember that you are unlikely to be assessed on *what* you have read; more important is the use to which you can put that reading.

Some of my students have benefited from structuring their reading by using a set of questions enabling them to focus on the relevance and usefulness of texts as well as to challenge what is being said and the way in which it is expressed. For example: What does the writer mean here? How can I use or adapt this idea in my professional work? Does the evidence justify the claims that the writer is making? You might formalize this procedure into a list of questions that you pose every time you read an article or book. While this may seem cumbersome, and perhaps even restrictive, my students have claimed that this method did enable them to focus their reading in a consistently critical way.

Whatever method you use, your reading of any article or book should be not only about understanding what results or findings have been presented, but also about working out:

- the ideas which are the driving force behind the article or book;
- how the author comes to choose what to put into the text and what to leave out;
- how the author comes to choose the particular style of presentation;
- whether or not the author's assumptions and conclusions are realistic in terms of your own professional experience;
- what directions and further problems arise from the work and if they are in any sense resolvable within your own professional context;
- any patterns (of difficulty, kind of question or way of questioning) that are becoming apparent as you extend your reading of the literature within the area.

The point is, of course, that you need to see reading the literature as more than just a way of gaining information. It is also an opportunity to learn how to interpret findings and events in your own experience and how to write in a style which is acceptable within the academic arena. A parallel notion is suggested in this book where we discuss what you can learn from the good public speaker about the art of giving lectures as well as learning about the content of the talk.

Checking against previously submitted work

When you come to write a major piece of work such as your dissertation or thesis, it is important that you check out what kind of work has been successful in the past. Most university libraries will hold dissertations and theses submitted successfully for higher degrees, and these can usually be viewed fairly easily. Clearly, you have to be careful in making judgements when looking through old dissertations and theses because you will not know necessarily which of the collection were exceptionally good and which just managed a pass (and, though it may not be widely acknowledged, there is such a distinction even at PhD level). Even when writing a minor assignment it may well be helpful for you to look at samples of work that have been successfully submitted at the level at which you are currently studying. The same caveats about level of success of previous work still apply; nevertheless looking at a range of previously submitted work (if that can be made available) will give you a feel for kinds of expectation.

The purpose of looking at previously submitted work is for you to begin to judge the kind of quality that is required at the level you have entered and to begin to gauge expectations of markers with regard to level of attainment in terms of quantity (number of words allowed) and kinds of presentation (use of devices such as diagrammatic representations, style of referencing, formality of prose). In many discipline areas it is also useful to begin to get a feel for the range of studies that fall within any one disciplinary area. You may well find that when you return to study after some years away from it, your subject has changed direction or expanded or become inextricably linked to other, previously distinct, areas of intellectual concern. Again, interdisciplinarity has increasingly become a feature both of professional work in the real world and of academic endeavour. Often courses of study reflect this increasing concern to see the links between disciplines; and modular structures lend themselves to interdisciplinarity as a framework within which you can develop your understanding of the world and particularly of your professional work. Looking at current submitted work enables you to orientate yourself to the concerns, limits and connections of your own and related discipline areas.

Making and using notes

Your own use of notes

Notes are made and used in professional life for a variety of reasons, and it may be useful to recall your own experiences.

Reflection: Your own use of notes

If you have made notes in the past then have you done so with a conscious intention to use them again in the future?

Have you made as much use of your notes as you thought you would at the time of making them (and if not, why not)?

Have there been distinctions between the kinds of notes you have made in your professional work as opposed to those made during your previous experience of academic study?

▶ **Student responses**

My note-taking has been deliberate: sometimes through habit, sometimes to keep focused, sometimes to sort thoughts out when reading.

(Education consultant)

My professional notes are more concise, I extract only the relevant information whereas before (as a student) I would write down everything.

(Medical engineer)

Professional notes are legal documents. Academic notes used for study can be rough.

(Midwife)

If it seems that notes have not been particularly useful to you, then clearly you need to reconsider how their effectiveness can be improved for you, or indeed if taking notes is worth the effort in the first place. If there are distinctions between the way in which you have used note-taking in your professional as opposed to your academic work then it may be worth considering why those differences have arisen and why one form of usage has proved more profitable for you than the other. For example, it may be that your professional note-taking has tended to be more purposeful and defined and used more directly and specifically than the kinds of notes which many undergraduates take and which are taken randomly and used sporadically, if at all. Notes that may later attain the status of legal documents clearly warrant a particular level of attention.

Taking notes during lectures and from reading

Many students try to use note-taking too exhaustively in their studies. Trying to write down virtually every word that a lecturer utters is unlikely to be helpful because you are likely to end up losing the overall sense of the content of the lecture in your efforts to capture the detail of what is being said. It may be more helpful for you to listen to a talk, or sections of a talk, and subsequently make short comments summarizing the import of what has been said. Here, of course, you are dependent to a certain extent on the ability and willingness of the lecturer to structure the content of his/her lecture so as to make it amenable to being tackled in this way; also, there has to be some sense in what is said if there is to be sense in what you write about it.

It may be that summarizing what you have read is most useful to you if it is in the form of written notes which précis the original in continuous prose. However, it is more likely that the meaning of the text in front of you will be more accessible in future if the prose is broken up into headed subsections in that subheadings allow you to find your way around your notes at a later date. Indeed, it may be that breaking down your notes into single words and phrases is most effective in terms of ease of recording and subsequent memory prompting. This kind of skeleton outline of what is presented in the text is probably the most popular form of note-taking. Headings and subheadings then become the significant tool for summarizing text; they also become a significant aspect of the way in which you rework the meaning in your head and make sense of it for yourself. As with taking notes during lectures, there is the danger, however, that in reducing original text to skeleton form you may actually lose your sense of the direction of the author's argument. So, it may be worthwhile to summarize your view of the overall message in one or two sentences. In this sense, taking notes becomes inseparable from your thinking about what you read.

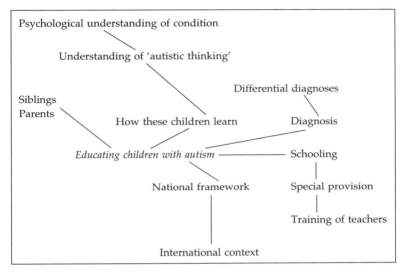

Figure 4.1   Example of patterned notes

An alternative to the methods suggested above is to develop a way of producing notes in a more diagrammatic form – often referred to as 'patterned notes', 'spray diagrams' or 'spider charts' – using key words to represent issues or concepts. The focus is still on setting down the key words as you understand them, but you begin by writing the main issue or concept in the middle of the page and connect subsequent concepts to that central issue with lines. When new points are made or concepts introduced by the speaker or writer which are connected to these subsequent concepts then you can link them accordingly, thus forming clusters around the periphery of the page. An example is shown in Figure 4.1

Importantly, the resulting spider's web of key concepts and connecting lines of argument should enable you to develop an understanding not only of the key issues but also of the way those issues are connected (by the speaker or writer if not in the real world of your experience). The advantage of this kind of system is therefore that it enables you both to record what is being said or written and to construct your own related framework of meaning at the same time. There are a number of variations on the basic spider diagram described above. Clusters can be connected to other clusters, arrows on lines can be used to indicate the direction of argument, connecting lines can be given more or less importance, comments can be written later to elaborate on your own understanding of (and challenge to) the speaker's or writer's ideas or content. Also, you may choose to make a linear set of notes in the first instance and then later turn them into a more diagrammatic form; in this way you may come to see connections in the lecture or the text (or perhaps disconnections) which were not immediately apparent as you listened or read.

Finally, on the issue of note-taking during lectures, it is possible to use a dictating machine of some kind and to record what the lecturer says for ease of reference later. This course of action should only be followed with the permission of the lecturer. The usefulness of a sound recording should not be overestimated, much will have been 'lost' in the reduction of the lecture to words on a tape (for example, gestures and use of diagrams) and reproductive quality may well be a problem – lecturers move around and direct their voices to different parts of a room and an audience is hardly ever still and silent.

Developing a bank of references

If you are involved in a substantial piece of work such as a series of experiments or a long essay or dissertation then you should be aware of the need for a structured way of recording what you read. Obviously, when an author cites something that looks interesting, you need to make a note of it. Early on in your studies you need to establish a bank of useful references and develop an effective system of cross-referencing that will enable you to find what you want without undue waste of time. You should not rely on your memory to recall the fascinating piece of information that enables you to answer a particular problem just at the time when you need it. The initial difficulty is in creating the kinds of categories that will sustain your particular academic work as it progresses. It is worth spending some time in developing a flexible yet robust system of cross-referencing based perhaps in the kinds of concern that are rooted in your professional practice. You might proceed as follows:

- Set down in note form what you require from a bank of references.
- Experiment with some categories that might form the basis of a cross-referencing system.
- Test out your system with some specific examples.
- Evaluate and modify.

In terms of some of the broader issues relating to making use of notes, you may find further guidance in Northedge (1990) and Rowntree (1988).

Summary

In this chapter we have considered:

- how to focus your reading on particular key texts and authors;
- strategies for making your reading more efficient;
- different sources of information, and their relative usefulness;
- developing your existing style of note-taking;
- developing a bank of references and experimenting with a system of cross-referencing.

Conclusion

Turning over half a library (see the quotation from Johnson at the start of this chapter) may seem a little excessive, especially when we consider the size of many current university libraries. However, it does help to recognize that reading is an essential prerequisite to setting pen to paper if you are to produce writing that can qualify as academic. Therefore the question that this chapter should have left you with is: how best can you structure your reading and note-taking so as to get the most out of your subsequent writing? A subsidiary question for you as a professional is: does reading for academic purposes differ in any meaningful way from the kind of reading you do in your professional life? Clearly, the answer to this latter question will affect the kinds of structures and strategies you choose to adopt and develop.

5

Planning to write

There is no use indicting words, they are no shoddier than what they peddle.

(Samuel Beckett, *Malone Dies*)

Overview

This chapter deals with the stage at which you engage in planning your written work. We will consider the preparatory and initial stages of producing written work, looking at:

- the process of writing as a part of the overall process of studying;
- the kinds of decisions you need to make in the preparatory stages of producing written work;
- some of the problems you may face in getting started on producing written work;
- the significance of constraints on word length for the way in which you write;
- how you may choose to structure your written work for your reader and use the process of structuring as a part of your overall strategy for effective writing.

Introduction

You may feel tempted to focus your attention on the act of writing and to see this aspect of your study as all important – after all, you are likely to be assessed primarily on your written work. However, as Samuel Beckett suggests in the quotation above, it is what you are trying to 'peddle' that is of primary import. Certainly, a weak argument can be made to sound stronger by a judicious use of prose, but it will remain a weak argument nevertheless. What is required of you is that you focus in the first instance on the message you wish to convey to your reader. The stage of planning to write is, therefore, all important.

A useful book that would supplement your reading of this chapter (and indeed the previous one) is Seal (1997); it deals with reading, study skills and writing.

Writing as part of the process of studying

You may have encountered a 'traditional' view of writing in academic work which suggests that it is something that takes place after content has been decided upon and after the thinking or the investigation has taken place. In short, you do your thinking, reading and/or empirical investigation and then you write it up. There is another view however, which suggests that the process of developing ideas and the act of writing them down as text need not be conceived of as separate and distinct activities. You will often find that setting down text forces you to clarify what you mean. Finding ways of expressing your ideas is, in part at least, a process of formulating those ideas or at least developing them further. This view is well expressed by Torrance and Thomas (1994).

Before you begin a piece of writing, you should put some thought into the purpose of it. On the one hand, you can conceive of it as expressing ideas for the consumption of an assessor; on the other hand, you may take a more formative approach and interpret it as part of the development of your ideas. Whatever your interpretation, it is reasonable to suggest that you need to start writing (albeit in rough) sooner rather than later in the process of completing any academic assignment. Word processors, with their facility for changing text, can help you to begin to write 'unformed' ideas with a view to their later development.

The early stages in academic writing

I have been influenced in my writing of this section by a number of texts, in particular: Hamp-Lyon and Courter (1984) and Weissburg and Buker (1990), – both of which offer good advice not just for researchers but for students in general.

Deciding on content

As a returning student you may feel somewhat overwhelmed by the task of writing for a particular audience in a particular style to a particular word length . . . All of these things are important, of course (and indeed they are considered in this chapter), but the primary concern is that you have something to say and that you know what it is. Often what seems to be a problem of setting down words that make sense is really a problem of not knowing what it is that you want to say. You may find that you need to take time out to think through what your content is to be and then go about setting it down simply and directly. Again, experience has shown that a common misconception in the early stages of returning to study is to assume that one of the purposes of academic writing is to sound clever. The main purpose is to convey meaning clearly, precisely and simply.

Setting the scene for the reader

In any piece of written work, it is important that you set the scene for your reader in order to help them find their way through your text. An obvious way to do this is to include a short abstract or introduction which summarizes what your text is about. This device can be used for essays, papers, technical reports, dissertations and theses. Certainly for the latter kinds of written submissions there is likely to be a formal requirement for an abstract, usually with a precisely defined word length. But there is nothing to stop you using the same method of scene setting in a short essay. If there has been some practical investigation that formed a part of the assignment (which is increasingly common in courses for professionals) then you need to summarize for the reader what was done, what was found and very briefly what the major implication is. To achieve this in one short paragraph is not an easy matter, but this does not lessen its importance. If there is no practical investigation involved then you need to summarize the main points that are discussed. The use of abstracts is revisited in Chapter 7. However, it may be helpful at this point to look at an example.

Abstract
The intention of this article is to examine three strands of research concerning the relationship between pupil cognitive style (as assessed by the Cognitive Styles Analysis) and the following factors: pupil performance in GCSE technology examination project work; teaching strategy; teacher and pupil motivation. The research was investigated with a sample of 112 15–16-year-old pupils (85 boys and 27 girls) selected from eight schools. Analysis of the data collected indicated that a pupil's cognitive style did affect their ability to perform in GCSE design and technology project work. The teaching strategy adopted was shown to have differing effects upon a pupil's performance depending upon the cognitive style of that pupil. The data also indicated that the relationship between a pupil's motivation and their teacher's motivation was affected by a pupil's cognitive style.
(Atkinson 1988)

Similarly, you should not be afraid to summarize content at the outset in diagrammatic form if that is appropriate. For example: a time-line might be helpful to your reader if the assignment reports events over a period; a map may be helpful if the problem is spatial: a 'family tree' may summarize complex relationships that are to be explored in the text, and so on.

Adopting the right tone

In part, finding the appropriate tone for a paper is a matter of adopting the conventions of academic writing (which are tackled in the next chapter) but it is also a matter of adapting to the particular culture within which you are writing. I am using the term – here, 'culture' should be understood in both its macro (in my case the UK) and micro (the specific culture of the discipline concerned) senses. For example, in the UK findings tend to be written up in a non-assertive way, and in the sciences writing tends to revolve around evidence and proof. Within this kind of culture you would be unwise to try to 'sell' your work (as being, for example, startlingly innovative or offering genuine insights) or to neglect a rigorous analysis of what counts as evidence.

You should also bear in mind the kind of audience you are writing for. Certainly, your argument needs to be rational and any conclusions 'correct' if you are to achieve good marks, but an essay also has to be easy to read and understand. A common difficulty experienced by students is to rely too much on the reader doing some of the work for them. You should not expect your reader to make deductions regarding what you mean in your text, nor should you expect them to see through oblique statements and recognize the implications of what you have written. Always assume that the reader only knows what you have put in front of them. The problem for you as a writer is that while you may be immersed in your topic, your reader may not be so involved. You need, therefore, to point out clearly all that the reader needs to know without, of course, labouring the obvious points. Clearly, one way to do this is to put yourself in the place of the reader and try to see from their perspective what it is that they need to know in order to make sense of the text.

As well as the issue of tone, it may be worth noting here that if your writing is unclear them you may be confused about the nature of the question you are trying to answer. This issue will be discussed later in this chapter.

Blocks to writing

At some point in your course of study you may find it difficult to make progress with the writing of an assignment or a report. The term 'writer's block' is often used: this at least gives the impression that what you are suffering from is some common condition which is identifiable and therefore holds out the possibility of remediation at least or cure at best. In fact, of course, there is no such thing as writer's block *per se*. However, there is a set of problems that commonly afflict those engaged in the process of writing, and Table 5.1 lists some of them and offers some possible solutions.

Table 5.1   Blocks to writing

Problem	Comment
'Whenever I start to write, the words simply do not seem to be good enough.'	You need to see writing as a process of changing ideas in text. What you write at the start does not have to be the final product – word processors make it possible to write something inadequate at first and return to it later to make it right. Perfect writing is unlikely in any case, but it is certainly unrealistic to expect it at the first effort. What is needed is to start putting down some of the key ideas (without worrying unduly about form) and to use the process of writing to clarify those ideas and so in turn enable an easier flow of writing.
'I have a hopeless feeling that writing any kind of worthwhile text is beyond my immediate scope.'	Consider starting by setting down an outline (see the next section in this chapter) of what you intend to convey in the piece of work. Work from the broad outline towards finer detail until you have some sense of a specific subsection that can be begun.
'I assume that the assignment can and should be written from start to finish in sequential order and I am uncertain about what the starting point should be.'	Again, think about starting simply by writing down the key ideas that you want to put across. Then go back and think about writing the introduction (having clarified in your own mind what the project is actually about) or perhaps one of the later sections.

Many of my students over the years have told me that they work better under pressure (usually in response to my expressions of anxiety that they get on with some work) and that if they leave the work until the deadline looms then the necessary pressure will naturally occur. It is probably true that your professional life is a busy one and that sometimes work necessarily has to wait until it can wait no longer. But to suggest that one works 'better' under pressure is, I think, largely a matter of self-delusion; the fact that many students end up working under pressure does not necessarily make it a better way for them to work. Certainly, academic writing requires reflection if it is to be effective and that reflection requires time, but you need to see the process of writing as inseparably linked to the process of thinking – starting to write early is likely to improve the quality of your thinking and hence of your writing. One of the problems for you as a professional returning to study is likely to be that there are always going to be reasons for not starting work on an assignment 'now'. Hard though it may be, you need to try to distinguish between real reasons and your own prevarication.

For more thoughts on writer's block you might wish to take a look at Hall (1994).

Choice of title (assignment brief)

Increasingly, students are given a choice of assignment brief in their course of study, and we assume here that such a choice exists. If you are having difficulty in getting started on an assignment then it may be worth reconsidering the assignment title you have chosen. You may find, when you think about it, that you chose it for the wrong kind of reason. Perhaps you chose it because it looked the easiest of the ones available, or because the majority of the group chose it. If you choose for the wrong reason then it may be that you will not be as committed to, or as interested in, the topic and might find that you lack the motivation necessary to sustain you in the work. So if you do encounter difficulties perhaps you need to question yourself about why you have chosen as you have and remain aware that your reluctance to make a start may be because you are not convinced that a particular title is of interest, or of use, to you.

There is one important caveat to the last sentence of the previous paragraph: students from a professional background sometimes insist on tackling assignments *only* if they can see an immediate professional relevance. While it is reasonable to want your study to contribute to your professional development, gain in this sense may not always be immediately apparent. Whatever your professional context, it is likely that a range of skills and knowledge will be required, not all of which are identifiable at the outset. Being a professional means being able to bring different abilities to bear on a variety of situations, and importantly it means knowing what skills are required of you and when. This is in contrast to a non-professional context, in which predetermined skills and knowledge are applied within a narrow sphere of operation with largely predictable outcomes. So, to define what is professionally relevant is rarely a precise art, and in turn to choose only to engage in study activities with a direct and identifiable gain is to ignore some of the crucial aspects of professionalism.

Your choice of title may often revolve around reasons other than professional relevance, such as what is thought to be already known ('I feel safe with the familiarity of this topic'), availability of relevant texts ('I know where I can lay my hands on books about this subject') or a relationship with a particular set of beliefs or opinions ('I feel strongly about this topic'). While none of these reasons is necessarily wrong, each may present you as a writer with difficulties:

- Previous experience with a particular problem or subject area may limit your progress in that you can be hampered by existing preconceptions. The problem you have in your mind may seem the same as that expressed in the title on the page in front of you, but appearances can be deceptive and you may find your responses to the new problem predetermined by your past experiences.
- Availability to you of relevant texts can be important; but equally, if you always depend on the known you are hardly likely to broaden your horizons.
- Returning to academic study should be about challenging your professional beliefs. If you embark on an assignment intent on proving what you have come to 'know' in your professional practice then it is quite likely that you will have difficulty in

producing critical, thought-provoking text. Whereas examining, for example, *why* you have come to operate in your professional work according to a defined set of beliefs in the way that you have and what the effects of such belief-based operation are on you and your clients at least holds out the possibility of critical appraisal of a professional belief system in action.

Understanding the title or question

A common difficulty arises when the meaning of the question is not clear or when students are not confident in their interpretations of it. Some possible reasons for apparent task difficulty and some possible responses from you as a student are given in Table 5.2.

Understanding the title before you start writing is crucial to your success in addressing the issues which the title requires. Certainly, failure to address particular aspects of the assignment title or report brief is a common reason for low grades. Markers comment all too often that the student appears not to have read the question or has written a good answer but unfortunately not to the question which he/she was supposed to be addressing. An interesting perspective on questions and titles is given by Mullarkey (1993).

Word length

It is important to note carefully the length required before planning your assignment and of course to consider the implications of the required length in terms, for example, of what you will be able to cover. Usually word length is given in thousands of words and as a maximum. Firstly, then, you need to be able to translate 'thousands of words' into whatever system you are using (so that if you tend to count in pages then you need to figure out roughly how many words you get to a page). Most word-processing packages have a word count facility which you should find useful. There is little gain and a lot of potential frustration in finding that you have written far too much on the early stages of a paper and not left yourself enough words for the later, and perhaps crucial, parts. Secondly, you need to interpret the requirement

Table 5.2 Understanding the title

Apparent difficulties	Responses
'Some of the terminology is unfamiliar to me.'	If it really is a matter of terminology alone then simple clarification of terms should be all that is necessary. However, uncertainty over terminology may mask a lack of understanding on your part at a conceptual level (in which case see below).
'I do not understand some of the concepts that appear in the title.'	Inasmuch as learning a subject is to some degree a matter of learning the language of that subject, then it may be that particular terms are being used to describe concepts with which you *are* familiar, in which case, again, clarification of the way in which terms are being used is what is required. If, on the other hand, your uncertainty is really at a conceptual level (if you cannot reduce the words of the title to a form which retains sense and which you do understand), then you need to read around the subject before you start writing in order to try to get clear those concepts that are initially elusive.
'The intention behind the wording of the title seems obscure to me.'	Ask yourself if the title is written in such a way as to render it obscure (and if this is the case, whether or not this is deliberate on the part of the tutor) or if your reading of it is in fact at odds with what is actually said (in which case you need to rethink your own interpretation).
'The title requires me to make use of material with which I am unfamiliar or to which I have an aversion.'	You need to consider how significant your unfamiliarity is or the extent to which your aversion is based in any real lack of skill or knowledge (and how readily that can be remedied).
'The title asks me to complete a task in a word length or time span that seems unreasonable.'	You need to recognize that word length is a constraint that applies to all candidates and is part of the rigour of the task - a further analysis of just how the task can be completed within the constraint may be helpful.
'The title is in the form of a question and I am not certain of the answer.'	Questions do not always require a straightforward positive or negative response – it could be that you are expected to come up with an answer, but that any such answer may necessarily be conditional on various factors or may require a caveat.

accurately; if it says 'maximum' on the assignment sheet then it means precisely that. It does not mean that you have to write exactly the number of words given, but it does mean that you should not exceed the limit set. You should note here that many tutors will comment that the best assignments are often the most succinct.

Many schemes will require the marker to penalize a student who writes an excessive number of words in completing an assignment. While you may think this draconian, it does make sense if part of the rigour of the task is to give an answer within a length constraint. After all, academic writing is all about clarity and brevity. Penalizing for excessive word length is thus fair and proper. One can argue, of course, that valuing such features in writing is also a good preparation for professional life where, as a general rule, professional reports and the like are valued for their clarity and brevity. In any case, constraints on word length are there for a purpose and it is vital that you recognize and adhere to them.

I will return to the topic of word length in the next chapter, where ways in which you can cut your text to meet word length criteria will be considered.

Appropriate format

Generally the form in which you will need to present your assignment will be driven by the nature of the content involved. Remembering that the underlying purposes of academic work are to convey meaning as accurately and accessibly as possible, then clearly the use of, for example, graphs and tables will be useful in certain contexts.

Dividing up the task

If the task that you face seems daunting in terms of its sheer magnitude then you may be able to find ways of dividing it into easily manageable components. It will be easier then for you to see a place where the task can be started and a way of managing the whole by taking one piece at a time. For example, you may

Reflection: Focusing on the task (assignment brief)

To focus on the task, ask yourself:

1 What is required of me in this task?
2 How can I best (that is, most effectively in terms of clarity and brevity) get across to the reader that I have understood the task, have completed it satisfactorily, have learnt from so doing and have developed my professional understanding and skill in the process?

▶ **Student responses**

I usually try to repeat the question somehow at the end, putting it into my own words and fitting in my answer as well.
(Industrial manager)

I have learnt to start by writing down in a couple of sentences on a card what the project is all about. I keep the card to remind me as I go what I am supposed to be doing.
(Environmental scientist)

I sometimes start an essay by stating what I think the thing is about and what I will therefore need to cover to deal with it.
(Therapist)

be able to divide up the task simply in terms of: the parameters of the problem as you see it; the practical steps you took to resolve it, in chronological order; your reporting of the results; your analysis and discussion of those results; your evaluation of all that has gone before; and your conclusions. What was an open and potentially confusing situation becomes a solution in six parts. Once you have divided up the task, you can begin to think of the proportions of the words available to you that can be devoted to each of the sections.

This notion of dividing up the task may seem attractive and may prove useful. But there is an attendant danger (which mirrors the difficulty noted in Chapter 2 where I discussed the possible loss of synchrony when a problem-solving protocol is used to separate a process into discrete identifiable stages). In dividing up a task it is possible that you may lose your overall sense of purpose and direction, so you must try to retain an overview of what the task is about and how the parts that you create for the purpose of structuring your work actually fit together. To this end, it may be worth your while building into your 'divisions' limits on word length or on the time you will spend on writing the individual parts, so that the resulting paper remains balanced.

On this last point, when planning the task ahead and using strategies of dividing up activities into components it is often helpful to consider the rate and pace at which you intend to work. This is very much an individual matter: some students prefer to work effectively in set and substantial periods of time, while others feel more comfortable with shorter periods of activity. Whatever mode of operation you adopt, the pace of your work needs to be matched to the way in which you have divided up the task. As many students have recalled from their experiences of taking examinations, leaving little time for the setting down of key issues having spent overlong on secondary matters can prove a costly error.

Developing a structure for your assignment

Getting started

Developing a structure for your assignment is part of the way in which you can usefully divide up the task ahead of you. There are a number of different ways of beginning to plan the structure of any written piece of work. We will consider two extremes to illustrate the kind of choice that you have.

One approach involves taking a blank sheet of paper and quickly and randomly listing all the information and ideas that come into your head as possibly worth inclusion in your assignment (accepting that such a list will invariably not be truly random in that it will always reflect some kind of construction on your part). A little while later, you revise this list by excluding any material that seems, on reflection, to be extraneous to the assignment brief, adding where necessary and then grouping ideas together and finally putting them into an order which reflects a reasonable development of an argument or an answer to any question which is inherent in the brief. If you were to follow this kind of procedure you would be progressing from a random set of ideas to a coherent structure.

On the other hand, you may feel more comfortable with an approach which is both more sequential and more ordered from the outset. You might start by analysing what is required of you by the assignment brief and then developing an outline from beginning to end (for example, 'I need to start by clarifying what is meant by X before I set about describing my own professional practice in relation to Y').

Clearly, these approaches are at opposite ends of a continuum and there will be numerous variations in between. Your choice of approach will reflect your own favoured learning style, but the important points to note are: first, that there is a choice; second, that no one approach is necessarily better than any other; and third, that while you may have a preference for one style it may help you in the long term to be able to think flexibly about different approaches for different occasions.

General purpose of outlines

Whatever approach you take to getting started, it is important that you try at the outset to develop an outline structure for your assignment and to reflect on it and refine it as you start to write. This outline should enable you to judge whether or not you will have tackled the key issues raised in the assignment brief and you should be able to see the shape of your paper as it will be developed. Typically you are likely to want to include the following:

- some kind of planned introductory section offering an analysis of the question to be considered;
- some signposting of the way in which you intend to deal with it;
- the main body of the paper, focused on your argument;
- your conclusion or set of conclusions;

• a summary of all that you have written and your final thoughts and indications about questions left unanswered and implications for professional practice and further study.

You may find it useful to number your headings and sub-headings (e.g. 2.1 and 3.4.2), even if you decide to remove the numbering in the final presentation of your text. This technique helps make the structure clear and also enables you to see what kind of status you are giving to the various sections (for example, the title of section 3.4 needs to subsume whatever is in subsection 3.4.2).

You would be advised to construct an outline *before* you start to write, because you will then be able to see more readily whether or not there is a sense of logic and balance in the way in which you intend to set out your work. This sense can be achieved in different ways, as will become apparent in the sections that follow, but whatever method you employ your reader needs to feel that there is some reason and deliberate purpose to the way the text is set out. An outline which gives headings and subheadings can reveal to you in this preparatory stage how your content is balanced and how clearly the various parts of your paper support a developing and coherent argument or description. Section headings should relate both to the assignment title and to sub-headings and the outline should be understandable; if it is confusing or repetitive or disjointed then it needs reconsideration. If your paper develops from a specified question through various arguments, or the presentation of different kinds of empirical evidence, and then returns full circle to the original question (a device which is discussed elsewhere in this chapter) then you need to make clear in the outline that this 'circularity' is deliberate, and subsequently you need to make this overt in the text.

In short, you will find that writing an outline enables you to clarify the structure of your paper. It should help you to focus your writing so as to follow through that structure and, importantly, make clear to your reader as he/she reads how your work is developing. Having said this, a structure should not be adhered to in the face of contradictions or inadequacies that become apparent as you write – clearly the initial outline will need to be adapted as your ideas develop in the process of writing.

The use of an outline at the preparatory stage is discussed by Hamp-Lyons and Courter (1984).

Some alternative ways of structuring written work

Set out above are the basic things likely to be included in your outline. But at the planning stage it is worth considering different ways of structuring a written assignment (see Table 5.3). Again no one way has universal superiority – it is a matter of choosing a kind of structure that is amenable to the particular assignment which faces you and is appropriate to your discipline. Neither are the ways suggested in the TABLE mutually exclusive – indeed, there is a clear overlap. The notion of going from the general to the specific and back to the general, which is adapted below, is described by Dane (1990); the notion of considering structure from the perspective of the writer is adapted from Sides (1992). Both of these books are useful sources of ideas on the subject of writing for an academic audience.

A common feature of the approaches given in Table 5.3 is the suggestion that it might be useful to revisit early parts of a paper later in the light of 'findings'. This holds true not just for scientific work, but for work in any academic discipline. After all, the reader needs to see how you have made sense of what you have discovered (be that in terms of scientific discovery or as a result of a review of a particular body of literature or derived from an analysis of your own experience). Completing the circle is a useful device regardless of discipline, and is something that can be planned for in the initial stages of planning to write.

Summary

In this chapter we have:

- considered the planning of written work as an integral part of the whole process of study;
- worked through some aspects of the preparatory stages to writing, including difficulties in getting started;
- considered pragmatic concerns relating to word length and ways in which you might structure your written work.

Table 5.3   Approaches to developing an outline structure

From general to specific to general
- Introduce the general context of the study. Describe any particular theoretical framework necessary for an understanding of what is to follow. Give any empirical context of the study and any specific hypotheses that are to be tested.
- Describe any participants, materials and procedures in a 'methods' section.
- Cite any data and offer analyses in a 'results' section.
- Discuss how the results relate to the hypotheses, and reconsider the empirical and theoretical contexts in terms of the analyses of the data.
- Return full circle to the general context and, again, reconsider in the light of overall findings.

Problem-solving
- Give the context within which the problem state exists.
- Describe that state, indicating all that the reader needs to know in order to understand your perspective on the problem and your response to it, including your reasons for engaging with the problem in the way in which you did (here you may need to include professional and/or ethical considerations).
- Describe your actual response to the problem (any methods, material, etc.) and give an ongoing analysis of findings.
- Summarize the results of your study in terms of the initial problem state and evaluate your perceptions of the problem, the way you went about tackling it, the significance of any findings for the problem and for you as the problem-solver (most probably set in the context of your professional development).
- Conclude with some thoughts on any limitations/strengths of your particular problem-solving approach and any implications for further problem-solving activity within the general context first described.

Writer-centred
- Describe how you came to the topic (this may involve an analysis of an aspect of your professional practice).
- Analyse your experience with aspects of the topic (perhaps taking themes to maintain coherence).
- Give your reader some insight and understanding relating to your experience.
- Conclude with implications.

Conclusion

If you are to make clear to your reader what it is that you want to convey then you must first be clear about that message yourself. The following chapter deals with 'effective writing', but such a notion would be somewhat hollow without a clear understanding on your part as to intended meanings and, of course, without some merit in terms of content. As Samuel Beckett suggests in *Malone Dies*, there is little point in blaming your words if they appear to let you down, without looking first at 'what they peddle'.

6

Effective writing

Writing, when properly managed (as you can imagine I think mine
is) is but a different name for conversation.
(Laurence Sterne, *Tristram Shandy*, Bk 2, Chapter 11)

Overview

In this chapter we consider the process of academic writing and
examine ways in which you can make your own writing more
effective; we try to unravel some of the purposes of writing
in academic study as well as set out points of technique and
convention. In particular, we will consider:

- ways to structure your writing so as to enable the reader
  easier access to your ideas;
- some of the conventions of academic writing;
- the interface between your own professional experience
  and the production of academic essays and assignments;
- the way in which your reading of professional and academic
  texts needs to feed into your written work;
- how to present your written work for submission.

Introduction

As has been noted in earlier chapters, the whole purpose of
academic writing is to convey meaning clearly and succinctly.

A reasonable model to have in your mind would be that when you write you are engaging in a kind of conversation with your audience, as Laurence Sterne implies in the above quotation. It is however, a conversation in which you cannot modulate your pace or your direction in the light of the things that your conversational partner says – you get no immediate feedback. Effective writing therefore requires that you be particularly considerate of your audience's needs.

Making use of structure

Dane (1990) and Sides (1992) address the issue of structure explicitly and would make useful supplementary reading. Also worth a look are Creme and Lea (1997) and Fairbairn and Winch (1996).

Building a structure around questions

The argument put forward in the previous chapter and restated here is that if you can create an outline of headings and subheadings then you may be more able to organize your argument and therefore your assignment. It is likely that the more apparent the organization is to your reader then the more accessible will be the ideas and information that you wish to get across. In some subject areas and for specific kinds of assignment it may be particularly helpful if you can structure your work around key questions (a simple example might be to use subheadings in question form such as 'Why Has the Financial Market Declined?' rather than 'The Decline of the Financial Market'). The advantage of this approach is that it may force you to sharpen up your work into a critical argument rather than leave it as a collection of pieces of information and opinion; but the disadvantage may be that the use of questions will lead your reader to expect answers from you which you therefore need to deliver (or explain why this is not, in your view, possible or desirable). If you decide to use a series of questions then clearly they should build one upon the other.

Paragraphs

Whether or not you employ headings and subheadings, the logical structure of your paper should be reflected in the paragraphs into which the writing is divided. Each paragraph needs to be self-contained. In essence there needs to be one idea that you are expressing in a paragraph, and the sentences in that paragraph should relate to that idea. A paragraph should be, therefore, a coherent entity. If it is anything other than that then your reader is likely to become lost in a meaningless maze of ideas and information. When reading through and editing work take every opportunity to cut any paragraphs that do not relate to the over-all meaning of the larger section and cut or move elsewhere any sentences within a paragraph that do not address the central idea of the paragraph. This may seem overly rigorous, but when reading a lot of academic text any examiner is reliant on the ideas being presented in discrete coherent chunks as well as logically and clearly. If the examiner cannot rely on your writing in this way then his/her access to your meaning will be diminished, and this will inevitably be reflected in any assessment.

Signposting

A feature of a successful conversation is that the speakers will give indications about the direction in which they wish to take the discussion. Similarly, giving clear indications of direction to your reader is significant, given that one of your main concerns in constructing your assignment should be to help that reader gain easy access to your ideas, findings and the information you wish to communicate. Signposting takes many forms, but the central notion is that you should tell your reader what they are about to read, let them read it as straightforwardly as possible, and then tell them what they have read. If your work is lengthy or particularly complex then the stronger the need for some clear indication from you at the outset of what is to follow. Your reader needs to have the main points that you are to cover set out and organized in advance of their reading. There is little more discon-certing for the reader of academic texts than to be plunged into a complex of issues with no introductory preamble that allows him/her to accommodate the ideas and information presented in a coherent and focused way.

Some conventions in academic writing

It would be unwise to give the impression that good academic writing is much different from good modern English usage in general. The basis of good academic discourse is to write clearly and concisely. Collinson *et al.* (1992) and Fowler (1990) contain some excellent advice. Indeed, the latter should remain at your side, along with a dictionary, whenever you write.

Writing in the third person

In academic writing it is usually taken to be important to be as objective as possible in dealing with issues. One way in which you can do this is to avoid writing in the first person ('I was involved in discussion . . .') and instead write in the third person ('the author was involved . . .') or use other forms of words which avoid the use of 'I' ('discussions took place in which . . .'). Such styles are generally accepted within many quarters of the academic community as enabling you to 'distance' yourself from your subject and create a feeling of objectivity. Certainly, as a general rule it is wise to avoid overuse of the first person in academic writing. Nevertheless, in some spheres of professional and academic work reflection on your own responses to situations is required and avoidance of the first person at any cost can lead to clumsy phrasing and in turn to unintelligible text. Indeed, in some areas the use of the first person is seen as a way of strengthening the writing and is advocated. Common sense and a sensitivity to context on your part therefore need to prevail. You would be advised to check out usage of the first person in written assignments with tutors and/or against any guidelines on style and format that are set in scheme or course documents.

(●) **Task: Writing in the third person**

Write down a short paragraph relating, from your own personal perspective, an incident in your recent professional experience with a brief comment on how you felt about it.

Rewrite the paragraph without using 'I', 'me' or 'my'.

Switching tense

The way in which you make use of tense can be a critical factor in whether or not your reader is able to understand readily what you are trying to say. A common problem in writing clearly, especially when dealing with the reporting of complex developments within a fast-moving professional context, is that of controlling your reporting of events in such a way as to maintain appropriateness of tense. Indeed, when writing about the work of others and the status of knowledge it is necessary to hold to a system. You should use the past tense when considering the conclusions of others – for example, 'Jones (1993) *showed* that . . .' – but when writing about concepts that are established (where there is at least no significant present controversy) and have been published in the past you should use the present tense – 'Autism *is* a pervasive developmental disorder'. Varying the tense varies the status you give to particular sources and particular kinds of knowledge.

It is argued by some that academic writing should invariably be in the past tense and that the present tense should be reserved for specific directions to the reader concerning the current text ('here it is suggested that all children with autism are likely to . . .') and any general conclusions which can be accepted as established for whatever reason ('it is clear that . . .'). However, you may find it more comfortable to write in the present tense and again, in some professional spheres, the kind of reflective practice that is required in academic study may involve use of the present tense at least in the introduction and the discussion sections.

It is important to try to establish a use of tense which is reasonable and which you then stick to throughout a piece of writing. It can be very disconcerting for the reader, as well as misleading, when tense changes without any apparent rhyme or reason.

The danger of using stereotypes and derogatory terms in writing

If you use a stereotype in your writing then you are in danger of conveying a misleading message or at least a message that confounds rather than clarifies an issue. For example, if you write 'A nurse has a duty to care for her patients' then you are potentially misleading your reader, since not all nurses are female. One way out of this is to use a form which includes, in this case, both genders ('A nurse has a duty to care for his/her patients'). Of course, while this is useful in some instances, it can easily become cumbersome and intrusive for both you as a writer and later for your reader ('A nurse has a duty to care for her/his patients even when he/she is burdened by the loss of, for example, his/her wife/husband/partner that has left her/him emotionally distressed'). Alternatives are to adopt the plural form ('Nurses have a duty to care for their patients'), or to drop the offending gender-specific pronoun ('A nurse has a duty to care for patients').

Of course, stereotyping is more pervasive and often more subtle than simply the use of pronouns. The use of terms which categorize in a derogatory way is culture-specific; what may be readily understood and acceptable in one cultural context may not be in another and may change over time. For example, in the UK today the terms 'man', 'backward children' and 'mothering' are considered politically incorrect in certain contexts and may well cause offence to some readers, and the terms 'human', 'children with learning difficulties' and 'nurturing' are preferred. As a writer of academic texts you need to consider the implications of any terminology you use, in order to avoid the risk of misinterpretation or misunderstanding.

It may help you to come to terms with stereotyping if you consider any particular examples of it within your own professional experience. For example, a student with a background in midwifery, when discussing the ideas in this book commented:

I think that by stereotyping a client you may treat them inappropriately, you may not fully understand their actions, for instance people say that 'Asian women have a low pain threshold' which can lead to inappropriate medical responses.

Miller and Swift (1989) deals with the specific issue of non-sexist writing in some depth.

Using jargon and specialized terminology

One person's jargon is another's everyday working vocabulary. As a professional returning to study you have to come to terms with the way in which specialized language is used within your profession and the relationship between this and the demands of academia. It is perfectly acceptable, indeed it may be necessary, to use technical terminology in the writing of assignments. Depending on the intended readership, you may or may not have to use a device such as a glossary to explain the terms that you need to use, but there are likely to be at least some terms which will be used commonly in your particular profession and which you can therefore use with impunity in a course designed by, and organized for, those within that profession.

What is less acceptable, in any discipline, is the use of convoluted sentence structures and obscure terminology, when simple structures and straightforward words can do the job just as well.

 Task: Using specialized terminology

Write a few sentences which include as many examples of your professional jargon as you can manage (accepting that you may wish to define the words as 'specialized terminology' yourself).

Rewrite those sentences using non-technical, non-specialized language.

Abbreviations and acronyms

Clearly, abbreviations, where letters are employed to stand for words (such as BBC for British Broadcasting Corporation) and acronyms, where a word is formed from the initial letters of other words (such as NATO for North Atlantic Treaty Organization) are generally in widespread use. Within your own professional field they may equally be prevalent, though here meaning may be restricted to those within your particular profession rather than universally understood. Whatever the case concerning your profession, the use of abbreviations and acronyms in academic writing takes on an importance beyond any predilections you may have for their general use in that they may enlighten or obscure your text according to the way in which you have used them.

Abbreviations and acronyms can be useful where you need to make continual reference to something that has a long or complex name and which is readily abbreviated into an easily recognizable form. Obviously some abbreviations (of professional bodies, for example) are commonly used and may seem therefore not to need explanation. Nevertheless you should not assume too much in this respect; terminology changes over time and there can be confusing similarities (for example, in the world of special schooling SLD has been used to refer to 'severe learning difficulties' and also by some to 'specific learning difficulties' – two terms with very different meanings). Therefore, it is always wise to spell out terms in full and give the abbreviation in parentheses at first use in any written assignment. Alternatively you could make use of a glossary. Both techniques allow you to use the abbreviation alone thereafter with impunity.

It may be that you decide to generate your own form of abbreviation for something that is not commonly recognizable (particular groups of subjects in an experimental investigation, for example). This is fine as long as the text remains understandable; if the use of abbreviations makes it harder for your reader to follow what is going on then it is counter-productive. Similarly with acronyms: they have the advantage of being more readily remembered than some kinds of abbreviation in that they should relate to something meaningful, but over-elaborate and contrived acronyms can be distracting and irritating.

Professional orientation of written work

If your course of study is professionally orientated then there are likely to be underpinning implications that your own professional practice will be improved as a result of your course of study. Your writing therefore will need to reflect the way in which such an improvement has been effected. Examiners tend to look for evidence that study of the relevant literature, the conducting of investigations and active reflection on practice have changed the relationship with students' professional context in a positive sense. This is not to say that direct evidence of being better at your job will be required of you in an academic assignment (though it may be) but that your understanding of your own professional activities and the way in which they relate to other connected aspects of the wider social setting has broadened and deepened and that the range of your professional skills has been extended. Further, an increased flexibility in your approach to problems and in the way in which you deploy your skills is typically seen as a desired outcome of such courses. In short, you would do well to try and show in your written work how your critical awareness has increased as a result of engaging in your particular programme of study (for example, that your awareness of new techniques in sampling might improve your performance as an environmental scientist or how an increased understanding of equal opportunities legislation might improve you abilities as a personnel manager).

Clearly, as well as highlighting professional gain by including reference to it in the content of your written paper, you need to write in a style that indicates that you have analysed your own practice in a critical and reflective manner. You need therefore to avoid description and anecdote in favour of analysis and the organized relating of events; you need to eschew opinion but offer considered reflection; you need, in short, to strive for objectivity.

Using your reading

The influence of your reading on your writing

Your written work needs to reflect what you have read if it is to lay claim to being based on anything other than your own 'untutored' views. As noted in Chapter 4, when preparing for an assignment you should try to focus your reading on that which is useful and relevant to the completion of the work. When you write the assignment you need to refer to the reading you have done, making it clear how your reading has influenced what you have written (this is not to say, of course, that you have to agree with everything that you have read).

If you do not refer to your reading as fully as possible when you write then you are not giving an indication to your readers that informs them about the range of your reading and, in turn, they cannot be expected to give you due reward for your efforts. There are two major reasons for showing your readers how you have underpinned your writing with evidence or reasoning from academic literature: first, as has already been noted, you want to be rewarded for your reading; and second, if you set down ideas or facts without acknowledging your source you open yourself up to accusations of plagiarism (see below).

Referring and quoting

In order to acknowledge the work of other authors in your text it is usual either to refer to their work or to quote their actual words. There is an important distinction between the use of reference and quotation, and again the relative value of their usage is open to some personal interpretation.

To refer to other authors in your text (see later sections for ways of doing this) is to acknowledge their work – for example, 'Jones and Evans (1998) described their findings in terms of . . .' or 'integration in this case worked only with the involvement of peers as well as the support of staff (Nind and Powell 1997)'. In these cases you are putting into your own words what other people have found or have written about. Remember the point made earlier about referencing relevant material that you have read in preparation for the assignment. If you read something but do not refer to it anywhere in your text then you have denied yourself the chance of getting due credit for your reading. Coincidentally, and perhaps inadvertently, you run the risk also of setting down as original to you ideas or information which you have gleaned from reading the work of others. The other reason why you need to reference is that it enables your readers to pursue ideas or information for themselves in the texts that you indicate. They may wish to do this solely for their own interest, or to check that you have interpreted the referenced author accurately, or to check that you have not simply copied out words from the referenced text – whatever their motivation, they must have the opportunity to trace your sources.

In contrast, the purpose of a quotation is to set out the exact words used by another author because those words sum up a point or a piece of information succinctly. When you use a quotation you are saying effectively that the words taken and reproduced in your work are of particular significance to your argument and cannot be reduced or improved upon. Do, however, avoid the over-use of quotations because they can disrupt the flow of your own text and irritate your reader, who will want to know what *you* think and how you have interpreted the views and findings of others rather than how accurately you can copy. The usefulness of quotations comes when they are used sparingly as indicators of the direction of your argument or to reveal thought-provoking aspects of other authors' writings.

Quotations usually do not count in determining the overall word length of your assignment (they are not your words and in a sense, therefore, are not a part of your submission), but you would be wise to check this in the regulations for your particular course of study. Some typical questions and some suggested solutions relating to the use of quotations are given in Table 6.1.

Plagiarism

If you use material from a source in another author's work without acknowledgement then you are guilty of plagiarism. There is a thin but clear line between what has been described above as the proper and advantageous use of other people's work and a form of academic cheating. To stay on the right side of that line you need to be scrupulous in acknowledging your sources. It is usual in the regulations that serve academic programmes to find clauses which require examiners to penalize, to a greater or lesser extent, students who plagiarize in their written work. In many institutions plagiarism means automatic failure.

Table 6.1   Using quotations

Possible questions	Possible solutions
'How much detail do I have to give at the end of a quotation?'	You need to give the author's surname, the date, and the page number(s): e.g. 'which illustrates the fluidity of the process' (Kenyon 1997, p. 14).
'Should I start each quotation on a new line?'	This is largely a matter of style. Usually a quotation less than about three lines long will be run on from your text, and enclosed in quotation marks. Longer quotations should start on a new line, be indented, and now quotation marks are no longer necessary. If you have more than one quotation appearing together, you will need to decide how best to show them: whether run on in the text as part of the text's normal sentence structure, or each starting on a new line.
'I find I do not need to quote the whole section from the author – the important bits are at the beginning and end of the paragraph. Can I cut the quotation down?'	Yes, as long as you do not distort the meaning of the original; the typical device is to use three dots to indicate a cut: 'In the cross-cultural comparison made in this study it is clear that religious belief was the significant factor . . . the significance was apparent to participants themselves'.
'I want to emphasize one bit of the quotation for my own purposes. Can I do this and, if so, how?'	If it is necessary for your use of the quotation it is possible for you to give an emphasis by italicizing or underlining the key word(s): 'the movement was driven by industrial relations *difficulties* rather than by . . .'; you do need to add in brackets after this kind of emphasis a note which informs the reader that the emphasis given is yours and not the original author's: ('emphasis added'); this is necessary because clearly you are adding to the original text in such a way as to possibly affect the original author's intended emphasis and possibly even his / her meaning.

For further thoughts on the way in which your reading should influence your writing see Northedge (1990).

The reference list and the bibliography

The importance of referring to sources in the literature has been noted above. In this section we examine how you might go about this. There are two basic ways of listing sources at the end of a written assignment: in a reference list and in a bibliography. Interpretations differ as to the way these two terms are used and indeed of their relative desirability; you will need therefore to refer to your own course documentation and guidelines for clarification on this point (there may, for example, be variant usages such as bibliographic references). Broadly speaking, however, a *reference list* contains works to which you have referred in your text or from which you have quoted (see the previous section). A *bibliography*, on the other hand, is a list of works which you have read and which have informed your writing (though you have not necessarily indicated instances of this in your own text). You will no doubt come across both reference lists and bibliographies in any reading you do in preparation for a written assignment, although in the work you submit you are more likely to want to include a reference list. As already stated, your readers need to be alerted to sources that are being used and given the opportunity to verify what you have done or to pursue points of interest in the literature. In some contexts it may be of minimal value for you to list other books you have read in the form of a bibliography, but it is unlikely that this kind of process is going to give you any credit with the marker – if you have read something that is worth the examiner knowing about then you should quote from or refer to it in the text and include it in the reference list.

Setting out a reference list or bibliography

Of the various ways to reference work in your text, the two most common are perhaps the author–date (or Harvard) system and the numerical system.

In the *author–date system* system you list your references at the end of your paper (after any acknowledgement of individuals or institutions who have facilitated your work; and before any appendices) *in alphabetical order of authors' surnames* (see the list of references at the end of this book). In the text you give the name of the author and the year of publication: 'the development of these techniques by Singh (1998) changed the way in which . . .', or 'techniques were developed (Singh 1998) which changed the way in which . . .'. Of course there are often subtle differences to this basic format, and these are noted in Table 6.2.

In the *numerical system* you list your references – in the same way as for the author–date system – at the end of your work *in the order in which you cite them in the text*: 46. R.F. Merton (1963) *Social Theory . . .*). The references themselves are replaced in the text by superscript numbers: 'the production of metals, aircraft building and armaments.[46]'). The advantages of this procedure are its simplicity, the fact that you no longer need to clutter your text with names and parentheses, and a possible improvement in the flow of your text, but the disadvantage for your readers is that they have to keep referring to a list at the end of the assignment in order to know which authors are being referenced.

There are various acceptable ways of setting out references, but their common purpose is to impose regularity on the way you present information, thus facilitating access to that information for your readers, and to provide enough detail to enable readers to track down sources for themselves if they so wish. Approaches to referencing differ across disciplines and institutions, and you should seek out guidelines within your own course or from your own tutor. In this chapter, for no reason other than my personal preference, we will use the author–date system described above to explore the remaining aspects of referencing.

The reference list

You will not be surprised to learn that there are many variations on the way in which author–date references are set out. A fairly standard method is offered in Table 6.3. However, it should be stressed again that academic journals may have a style of their own and your tutors may require the use of a different

Table 6.2 Referencing

Possible question	Possible solution
'What happens if I want to refer to more than one article written by the same author in the same year?'	In your text refer to, for example, Mackay 1996a and later Mackay 1996b (and so on if necessary); then in your reference list simply list the references in the a, b, . . . order (and including the a, b, . . . after the date as in the text).
'I find that I want to refer to the same source repeatedly in a short space. Do I really need to keep repeating the date every time? It seems cumbersome.'	In some circumstances you may get away with omitting the date in an oft repeated reference 'Wong (1998) refers to a particular form of intervention and goes on to describe some of the outcomes in terms of. . . . Wong also makes claims regarding . . .'. In this situation, however, you may need to reconsider whether or not you are being too dependent on one author. Alternatively, some small stylistic changes might do the trick: for example, 'she also makes claims regarding . . .' or 'in this work claims are made regarding . . .'. The other possibilities are to use 'ibid., or op. cit.' (see below).
'Similarly, I find that I am referring again to an author's work to which I have *just* referred. Should I continue to write Stanislav (1992) even though it is beginning to sound cumbersome?'	In these circumstances you can use 'ibid.' (an abbreviation of *ibidem*, meaning 'in the same place'); for example, 'Stanislav (1994) discusses the development of new malarial drugs . . . findings about the side-effects of the drugs give cause for some concern (ibid., p. 217)'.
'I find that I am referring to an article that I mentioned some time earlier in the essay. Should I acknowledge that fact?'	You may use 'op. cit.' (an abbreviation of *opere citato*, meaning 'in the work quoted') where you have referred to a work earlier in your essay; it is essential that you give sufficient information for identification: 'Stanislav (1994), 'op. cit., p. 217'.

Table 6.2 Continued

Possible question	Possible solution
'In the front of the book which I want to reference there is more than one date. Which one do I use?'	You need to note the date of the edition of the book to which you have referred (not the print-run date or the original publication date).
'I have read more than one author who has written about this particular aspect: should I list them all, and, if so, how do I do that?'	If you are saying that a number of authors have investigated a particular problem or perhaps have reached similar conclusions then you can list them together (usually in alphabetical but perhaps in chronological order if that suits your particular purpose): 'a number of authors have reported similar findings in this respect (Evans 1986; Sokhi 1994; Wheeler 1990).
'There are two authors of the article I wish to reference. Do I note only the first author or give both names?'	If there are two authors then you need to mention both in your text: 'Tadgerouni and Whitty (1997) suggested that . . .' or 'It has been suggested (Tadgerouni and Whitty 1997) that . . .'.
'There are more than two authors of the article that I wish to reference. How do I deal with that?'	If there are more than two authors then you need to use '*et al.*' (an abbreviation of *et alii*, meaning 'and others') in your text: 'Lecourt *et al.* (1986) describe the way in which . . .'. If there are not too many authors then you might wish properly to list all of them the first time you note them in the text: ('Lecourt, Maggerote and Peeters (1986) describe . . .') and then use *et al.* for any further references. However, even if you use *et al.* in the text, you must list all the authors (however many there are) in the reference list at the end of your work.
'Do I use first names as well as surnames when referring to authors?'	Not without good reason – for example, you are citing two or more authors with the same surname whose works were published in the same year.

Table 6.3 Setting out references

Kind of source being referenced	Format for setting out
Single-authored book	Donaldson, M. (1978). *Children's Minds*. London: Fontana.
Edited book	Zuckerman, H., Cole, J.R. and Bruer, J.T. (eds) (1991). *The Outer Circle*. New York: W.W. Norton.
Chapter in an edited book	Blackman, D.E. (1984). The current status of behaviourism and learning theory in psychology, in: D. Fontana (ed.) *Behaviourism and Learning Theory in Education*, pp. 3–14. Edinburgh: Scottish Academic Press.
Single-authored article in a journal	Wing, L. (1981). Asperger's syndrome: a clinical account. *Journal of Psychological Medicine*, 11, 115–29.
Multi-authored article	Atkinson, P.A., Reid, M.E. and Sheldrake, P.F. (1977). Medical mystique. *Sociology of Work and Occupations*, 4(3), 307–22.

system which may employ full-stops, commas, colons, semicolons, brackets, italics and the positioning of the date in ways which differ from the method given in the Table. The important thing is to aim for consistency and clarity and, of course, to meet any criteria laid down in course regulations or by individual tutors.

Two minor points should be made here about references. First, in the light of our earlier observations on the use and misuse of abbreviations, it is unwise to abbreviate the titles of journals in your reference list. Second, italics and underlining to highlight the location of your source can be taken to be interchangeable (you can use whichever is easiest for you *as long as you are consistent*: what you need to do is locate precisely the part of the reference which tells the reader where to find the particular text being quoted or referenced).

Creme and Lea (1997) give further guidance on enhancing your abilities as a writer.

Presentation and submission

Addressing word limits

We will now return to a topic touched upon in the previous chapter and consider some ways of cutting your text so as to meet any limits on word length that may be set down in your assignment brief. There are various tactics that you can employ:

- Take out any unnecessary background information (you only need to tell your readers what they need to know in order to judge your response to the subject).
- Take out any unnecessary sections that define aspects of the subject in hand (think through carefully what you can reasonably assume the reader already knows).
- Reduce the amount of description surrounding the main issue.
- Consider if tables, lists, diagrams and the like can be used instead of prose.
- Look closely at the introduction (experience has shown that it is here that verbosity may lurk).
- See if any whole paragraphs can be omitted without losing the overall sense and without lessening the impact of the work in terms of answering the question.
- See if you can précis any whole paragraphs into one or two sentences.
- See if any two paragraphs can be merged and reduced by combining points into one meaningful issue.

Clearly, how you cut will depend on a whole range of issues relating to the kind of assignment and the way in which you went about addressing the issues in your first draft, but a good general piece of advice is to step back from the writing and ask yourself what you need to say and whether everything you have written is absolutely necessary to get across what you need to say. Cutting text may involve a certain amount of mental anguish but will often result in a much improved piece of work.

Avoiding errors

The point has already been made that your written work needs to convey meaning clearly and directly, and it follows that anything that interferes with this should be avoided. Errors of spelling can be irritating for the reader at one level and significant in terms of loss of meaning and comprehensibility at another; similarly, errors of punctuation can make text impenetrable or inaccurate. Both these sources of error are a frequent subject of examiners' comments.

 Task: Ambiguities and inaccuracies

See if you can identify the errors in the piece of text below and any ambiguities or inaccuracies that arise. Rewrite the piece without the errors.

They had walked down too the plane making sure that they kept his heads covered all the time: at midday they found some refuge from the topical sun under a three it was very hot when they arrived their Blankets were not necessary at all evening through, the nights were much cooler.

Here is one possible answer:

They had walked down to the plain making sure that they kept their heads covered all the time. At midday they found some refuge from the tropical sun under a tree. It was very hot when they arrived there. Blankets were not necessary at all, even though the nights were much cooler.

It is always a good idea to check your work by, at the very least, reading it through to yourself. Be sure to focus on what you have actually written, and not what you *think* you have written. In addition, most word-processing programs incorporate grammar and spell checkers which can help you. Be aware, however, that grammar checkers have considerable limitations and that spell checkers cannot catch every error you make – most obviously, when you misspell one word as another. You should not, therefore, rely on them to the exclusion of other means of checking.

Footnotes

The use of footnotes varies across disciplines. Where used, their purpose is to provide supplementary information for your reader, without interrupting the flow of the text, and as such they should not be required reading – that is, they should not be essential to an understanding of your argument.

The usual way to indicate a footnote is to put a superscript number at the appropriate place in the text. Most word-processing packages will have some kind of facility that automatically places the relevant footnote at the bottom of the correct page; however if you are not using a word-processing program then you will need to take great care when amending text to make sure that the footnote remains at the foot of the appropriate page.

Endnotes

One way round the difficulty of placing footnotes on the correct page and of restricting their size to a reasonable proportion of the page itself is to use superscript numbers in the text referring to notes at the end of the chapter or assignment. As a device this may be less attractive for your readers in that it requires them constantly to refer to a different place in the document but it does give you as the writer more space and flexibility. Again, notes used in this way should be non-essential to an understanding of the text itself. Note also that, since superscript numbers are also used in the numerical system of referencing (see above), if you use this system then any endnotes you may want to include could be neatly integrated with your references.

Appendices

In an academic paper it is more likely that you will use some kind of appendix than the endnotes described above. Again, the purpose of an appendix is to provide your reader with background evidence or material – for example, raw data, original notes, source documents or transcripts. The material in the appendix should be referred to in the text, usually in a form such as '(see Appendix 3)'. If your assignment involves some kind of investigation, as is often the case in professionally orientated courses, you should try to include in the text only summaries of any data collected and consign the bulkier 'raw' data to an appendix.

It is commonly accepted that the same point about essential reading applies here as it does in the case of footnotes and endnotes: appendices should not contain reading that is necessary for the reader to understand the argument. Examiners will expect to have to refer to an appendix only to find supporting evidence for the judgement they are to make about the quality of the work – not necessarily to make that judgement itself. Typically, appendices are not included in word length, but tutors are usually unimpressed by a huge appendix that dwarfs the actual paper; indeed, some course regulations ban over-large appendices.

Having pointed out the limitations on the purposes of appendices, it should be stressed that they can be an extremely important part of a written assignment. Indeed, some markers scan through the appendices before they read the main text to give themselves a feel for the empirical work or background material that supports the paper itself. It is important therefore that you organize any appendix carefully so that your reader can gain easy access to the relevant information. An appendix may be of an appreciable size (for example, a collection of data sets presented in tabular form and spread over a number of pages), so you need to find a way of numbering appendices in such a way as to retain coherence and yet enable easy access for your reader. You can achieve these aims by using physical devices such as tabs or coloured sheets to demarcate the various appendices. Another way might be to number the pages of the appendices separately from the main text (for example: A1, A2, . . .).

Again, you would be wise to check out the regulations for your particular course, especially when you come to the dissertation or thesis stage where more is at stake. Also, it may be possible for you to examine copies of successful assignments from the past (many institutions keep such copies for reference). Look at what kind of material is contained in the appendix and how the writer informs the reader about how to locate information in it. Such a search seemed to help one returning student (a primary school teacher) who commented:

> I found two appendices which were totally different: one was very well organized and I found it interesting in its own right; the other was like a dustbin for odd bits and pieces, it had photocopies of documents, children's work etc., but it all seemed random – I don't think some of it was mentioned in the text at all.

Summary

In this chapter we have considered:

- the structuring of written work and the need to help the reader through the text by means of 'signposting' devices;
- the usefulness of some of the conventions of academic writing such as writing in the third person and the deployment of tense;
- the dangers of using stereotypes, technical terminology, abbreviations and acronyms;
- links between academic writing and professional development;
- effective quoting and referencing;
- how to prepare written work for submission by minimizing your errors and maximizing your accessibility as a writer.

Conclusion

In this chapter we have dealt with the process of academic writing. We have looked at ways in which you can make your own academic writing more effective, the implication being that this will also have a positive effect on your writing within your professional context. Laurence Sterne, in *Tristram Shandy*, conceptualized writing as 'conversation': you would do well to treat your audience with the same kind of consideration that you would offer to conversational partners, taking into account what those partners already know and what they need to know in order to understand what you wish to say.

7

Writing a dissertation or report

An intellectual is someone whose mind watches itself.
(Albert Camus, *Carnets*, 1935–42)

Overview

Most courses in higher education include the production of a major piece of work. In this chapter we deal with this particular stage of your studies. We will consider:

- the purpose behind the writing of a dissertation and the kinds of demand it is likely to make on you;
- the way in which you will have to generate and control the questions which will underpin the dissertation;
- the need to focus and to plan and develop your work within particular constraints;
- the relationship between your dissertation work and your professional practice;
- the title and the abstract of your work.

Introduction

Your programme of study may culminate in a substantial piece of work in which you are expected to show how much you have learned. This work will often carry a heavier weighting than your other assignments when the marks for all your work are aggregated into a grade or classification; indeed, it may be that you can only get a good overall grade or even pass the course if this piece displays a particular set of required skills, more or less discipline-specific, and is considered to have achieved or exceeded a given standard. One of the first things you need to do is read the course documentation carefully to find out just what it is that this final piece of work is designed to enable you to demonstrate. There will be a purpose behind what you are required to do, even if it seems obscure – your task is to try to understand what is expected of you.

You might wish to supplement your reading of this chapter by looking at Hampson (1994).

The demands of a dissertation or report

You may find that this substantial piece of work is described as an extended essay, extended case study, project, portfolio, report, dissertation or thesis. To confuse the issue, a portfolio would contain a number of pieces of work, one of which might be considerably more substantial then the rest (and carry the name of one of the other items in the above list). Generally speaking, the term 'thesis' is usually restricted to research degrees which are awarded solely on the basis of investigations carried out by the student and written up as an argument which is then defended in an oral examination (commonly known as a 'viva'). For the purposes of this chapter, therefore, I will use the term 'dissertation'.

Before leaving terminology, it might be helpful to say something more about the difference between a thesis and a dissertation. Where 'thesis' implies the setting up of one or more propositions to be defended, 'dissertation' implies some detailed discourse on a given subject. You should not assume, however, that a dissertation would exclude the setting up of propositions; indeed, interpretations vary as to the extent that argument is seen as an essential part of a dissertation. It is important to find out from your course documentation, or through discussion with your academic tutor, just what is required of you at the dissertation stage. There is, however, a risk of underestimating the task if you assume

that all that is needed is a larger essay than those you have previously done. This is unlikely to be the case: knowledge and skills
learnt throughout your studies are likely to be brought together
for scrutiny by new assessment criteria – or criteria in which
there has been a subtle but significant shift of emphasis.

Whatever specifics your course documentation decrees, the final
piece of work in any course of academic study related to professional development is likely to require you to demonstrate not
only what you have read and what practical investigations you
have carried out, but also that you have become critically reflective about what you have learnt about your own professional
abilities and practices.

Questions to be investigated

Generating the question to be investigated

In many courses of advanced study, and particularly those which
engage with returning students from the professions, the theme
that runs through the various course components and culminates
in a dissertation is that of investigation. Higher degrees invariably
involve some kind of research, and the specification of the question to be investigated tends to rest increasingly with the student
rather than with the course designers as the level of academic
study rises. This shift is an important one: the higher you go in
academic study, the more you will be expected to understand the
nature of questions and the boundaries within which they can be
asked, and you will need to be able to generate questions that
are reasonable and, when properly pursued, can produce worthwhile answers.

Staying focused on the question

The higher the level of academic study, then, the more you are
likely to have to work to define and refine your question. If you
are starting on a dissertation and you are not clear about what it
is that you are trying to find out then you are unlikely to be successful; even if your work is necessarily open-ended or involves

finding out how to clarify issues for investigation, it should nevertheless be possible for you to write down, in one or two sentences, the question that underpins your work.

 Task: The underpinning question

Write down on a card the question(s) underpinning your dissertation.

Pin the card above your desk for the duration of your work on your dissertation, referring to it occasionally.

If you feel, at any time, that you are no longer engaged with your original question then consider the reasons and the consequences:

- If your line of investigation has produced tangible progress, it may be necessary to revise the original question.
- If you feel you have gone astray, you may need to spend some refocusing on the original question.

▶ **Student response**

I got wholly off track in my dissertation. It came home to me when my supervisor pointed out at the end that my title suggested something completely different than what I had done. We had to rewrite the title; funnily, that in itself helped me to track back through what I had done and then I began to make sense of it all. I reorganized it in retrospect (and survived).

(Primary school teacher)

I thought that in my discipline (environmental biology) it was unlikely that I would stray from the path set down at the outset with my tutor – it all seemed pretty clear-cut. But when it came to it I did in fact begin to get results that made me ask slightly different questions from the one I started with. I guess it was more a matter of adjusting to results than changing direction but, looking back on it, the 'adjustment' was important.

(Biologist)

Try not to lose sight of the question as your work proceeds. If you started out trying to find an answer to one question, perhaps from your professional context, then you need to be clear that the methods you employed and the conclusions you were entitled to reach did relate to that question. Changing the question subsequently but without reference to your original intentions might alter the kinds of methods required and certainly would affect the kinds of conclusion you are entitled to reach. For example, if you started out asking about the 'effects of hospitalization on children's educational performance' but became side-tracked into considering effects on relationships with peers from within the school setting, then measurement of schooling results and conclusions about the need for consistency of approach between school and visiting hospital teacher would become less relevant. It is not that the latter issues are unimportant or in any sense illegitimate, but it is necessary to recognize that they are different. You could argue that the words 'educational performance' in the original question simply need restating as 'education', thus encompassing the wider issues of relationships which you might consider as important as, and in any case inextricably linked to, levels of performance. At one level, this is quite reasonable but it would require you to rethink the parameters of your study: quite simply, you would need to consider whether you can do justice to the broader question within the defined word length and whether you can access the necessary range of children to enable you to answer the new question satisfactorily and within ethical boundaries.

Of course, any notion of 'going astray' in a project is dependent on the kind of trajectory you began with. Changing direction has different connotations in different disciplines and methodologies. In action research, for example, change is an inherent, and necessary, part of the process, whereas in a series of scientific experiments a *post hoc* analysis might require a particular kind of justification. You need to ask yourself whether you are still addressing the issue or hypothesis that you began with. Whatever your area, staying focused has its merits. Certainly, as you develop your dissertation you will need to keep focused on the underpinning question and be able to explain how each part of your theorizing and practical investigation is helping you to work towards an answer. Again, it is worth stressing that in the final written product you will need to make that explanation overt.

The issue of understanding questions and their use in academic work is explored by Mullarkey (1993).

How sharp should the focus of a dissertation be?

It would be misleading simply to say that all academic investigation should be narrowly focused. Certainly some investigations will have a sharp focus, with a question to be answered or a hypothesis to be tested, but others will have a less distinct focus, consisting perhaps of a general problem to be solved or an issue to be explored. In any case it is useful to try to define your investigation as accurately as possible at the outset and, as already noted, to monitor your focus as you progress through the study. One way to proceed is as follows:

1 *Establishing an issue*. Describe the broad area within which your enquiry is to take place (e.g. 'women in active combat units') and thus set the parameters within which you will define the problem and subsequently the question that you will pursue.
2 *Identifying a problem*. Define more specifically the nature of the problem that your investigation will seek to resolve (e.g. 'there has been an increase in the number of women assigned to command positions in active combat units, and this may result in effects which military planners will need to take into account in any future conflict scenario') and thus begin to formulate what it is that you are trying to resolve.
3 *Hypothesizing*. Formulate a statement in the form of a hypothesis (e.g. 'there will be effects of assigning women to command active service units – these will range across a number of dimensions of which one will be levels of aggression towards the enemy of male subordinates') in such a way as to enable you to search for evidence to support or confound your hypothesis.
4 *Defining the question*. Set out your question in such a way as to enable a search for specific information (e.g. 'do levels of aggression towards the enemy in male subordinates during active combat change as a direct result of the assignment of a

female commander?'), and in such a way as to make possible a successful outcome to the asking of the question.

One of the issues arising from this process is that the original example given ('women in active combat units') could have taken any one of a number of directions. It could have looked at a number of possible effects on the women themselves, on the men, on the relationship between women and men (both in combat situations and outside them), on efficiency in any one of a number of dimensions, on overall career structures, on recruitment, on medical provision in battle situations, on armament requirements and so on. The inherent dimensions within any issue will only become clear as you start to write down the issue you wish to tackle, followed by the problem arising as you perceive it and the subsequent hypothesis or question that you think is both answerable and valuable. In short, clarification of your question at the outset and monitoring during the process are essential if your investigation is to hold together as a coherent response to a perceived problem. Again, in the final write-up the process of focusing that you went through should be apparent for your readers – they need to know why you did what you did as well as simply seeing the results of your endeavours.

Defining the limits of your intended dissertation or report

Many students find that narrowing down a dissertation in terms of its overall aims and scope is a particularly difficult process, and that working on smaller, often discrete, projects has not necessarily prepared them to know 'how much' is required of a dissertation. Experienced supervisors should be able to help you by defining limits, but for you to be better able to interpret their advice you need to try to get a feel for these limits by checking out in the library the kinds of scope that have been acceptable in dissertations in the past. In short, if you can find previously submitted dissertations in your area then you can learn from reading them what is acceptable in terms of scope as well, of course, as gaining insights into kinds of topic, ways of dealing with issues and matters of presentation. Perhaps you will find that dissertations are often more modest in remit than you might expect.

What does academic investigation entail?

To supplement your reading of this section you might like to refer to Rowntree (1988), which offers excellent advice on clear thinking and a systematic approach. For those working in the social sciences, Phelan and Reynolds (1995) is a useful text.

Clear purpose

Investigations should have a clearly defined purpose, even when that definition indicates a very fluid and open-ended situation, for example: 'finding out what kinds of sculpture are made possible by specific new materials or processes arising as by-products of technological change'. If academic investigation is to have any value then it must at the very least be purposeful, and the purpose should be evident to the reader.

A systematic approach

There should also be a systematic quality to the investigation which is grounded in some kind of rationale or theory. Many disciplines will have a rationale that is central to their ways of working – for example, most natural sciences will have the possibility of replication as an essential aspect of any claim for valid 'new' findings, and all disciplines require investigations to subscribe to a rationale that provides a (typically logical) basis for actions taken. Indeed, this is what marks out a particular area of intellectual enquiry as a 'discipline' rather than simply a loose confederation of ideas. Of course there will be arguments about where disciplinary boundaries lie and about whether or not certain intellectual areas do in fact qualify as 'disciplines', and it will be helpful if you can locate your own discipline within these kinds of arguments because you need to be thinking about what counts as 'systematic' for you. If your professional work requires you to work across disciplinary boundaries, and if this interdisciplinarity is reflected in your academic study, then the matter of boundaries and the conventions that operate within them takes on a particular significance.

 Task: The rationale underpinning a discipline

If you can identify yourself within one intellectual discipline then note down some of its basic features. For example: what counts as data, as evidence or as proof?

Self-critical awareness

Implicit in any dissertation-level work is the need for you to exhibit self-awareness about the way in which your study was carried out and the implications arising from the kinds of choices you made in defining and pursuing your questions. Mistakes and disappointing results are less significant when you achieve high levels of critical analysis of the processes and procedures that you instigated and pursued in your studies. It may help to note that there are often two levels operating when examiners consider a piece of investigatory academic work: on the one hand, they want to know what has been found out and how significant that is; on the other, they want to know how much the student has learnt from the process of undertaking the work. This is why you should pay particular attention to explaining clearly why you did what you did and why you think that you found what you found and how undertaking all of the work has affected your own understanding of the problem itself, the methodologies employed and your own ways of working.

Advancing understanding

Your investigation will be expected to result in an advance in the current state of understanding in some way. It will not necessarily be a matter of making a significant contribution to knowledge: this requirement is usually reserved for the award of a PhD. But your dissertation will need to have shown, for example, clarification of the kinds of questions that need to be asked, the procedures that need to be followed to enhance a particular process, and the possibilities inherent in particular materials. A dissertation needs to inform the reader. The examiner ought, therefore, to be able to apply successfully criteria such as 'has reading this dissertation added to the way in which I understand the issue of . . . ?'.

Empirical and philosophical investigations

Throughout this section, there may seem to you to be an underlying assumption that the dissertation has involved some investigation 'in the field' resulting in empirical data (that is, data that relate to information gained through experience rather than from abstract reflection). It may be, of course, that your dissertation might investigate – or, perhaps more properly, interrogate – theoretical standpoints on a specific topic in the extant literature. In this sense your dissertation will need to add to your reader's understanding of that topic at an intellectual level that is not necessarily dependent on the collection and analysis of data. It would, however, be misleading to distinguish too rigidly between empirical and philosophical investigation. If you engage in empirical data-gathering then it is likely to be founded on conceptual understandings that may have been clarified at a philosophical level, just as any philosophical investigation you undertake might be based on an argument about how to clarify empirically based understandings. Thus while empirical enquiry requires data relating to questions or hypotheses, philosophical enquiry requires critical argument or debate: both require investigation.

Academic investigation and professional progress

The proactive profession

One of the essential bases of a profession is that it seeks self-improvement or at the very least seeks to accommodate to changes in society while retaining its integrity and its overall efficiency. In this sense your profession needs to be proactive rather than simply reactive to changes that occur, and the kind of proaction that is required if it is to survive and prosper needs to be based on intellectual reflection. It follows that if innovations in procedures, materials or processes are to be successfully integrated into the armoury of your profession then they need to be tested out rigorously by it in realistic situations which will indicate possibilities and implications.

It would be unprofessional to adopt an innovation that had never been reliably tested or that had no rationale to distinguish it from other new approaches. This would not be to say, however, that innovations are never adopted in this way. Indeed, when discussing the ideas in this book one student (a nurse) described her view of innovations as follows:

> The reforms in nursing began in the early 1980s. They were not scientifically thought through or piloted in some areas, with the consequence that they have to be amended. This is costly and damaging to patients. Resources were not provided in adequate amounts. Professionals in the area were fed up. This has deflected attention from some good aspects of change. Innovations are often politically motivated and this has not always been good.

Academic investigation (or, rather, investigation carried out within the academic context for an academic award) should mirror the kind of evaluation and examination that goes on in your professional domain. Of course, in an ideal world each would feed into the other: professional development would be influenced by findings from within academic contexts and academia in turn would be influenced by data and concepts derived from professional work in the field.

Identifying an agenda for change

It is not too pious to expect that if you engage in an academic investigation which relates to your professional work and results in some form of dissertation then that investigation should assist you in identifying an agenda for achieving positive change in your professional context. You should be able to use the investigation that your academic study requires of you to: clarify issues that are problematic in your professional work; unravel the implications and knock-on effects of contrasting approaches or the introduction of new materials; evaluate new ideas and practices in terms of their efficacy; and identify new directions for worthwhile future investigation.

Another key aspect of the professional and academic interface is the interdisciplinary dimension already discussed. Increasingly, professionals have to work alongside, or at least in the same arena as, colleagues from other disciplines and professions; if this is true for you then academic study should give you the opportunity to explore the boundaries of your discipline and to consider the way in which your profession can relate to others. Some of my students have told me that learning to talk to those from other areas has been to an extent a matter of contriving a shared language but that it has also been a matter of coming to understand the attitudes and driving forces behind the activities of other professional groups.

Dissertation constraints

When you come to decide on the form of your dissertation and on the kinds of investigation that will underpin it, you will doubtless have to consider carefully what you will not be able to do as well as what you will. Of course there are always constraints on any piece of academic work – indeed, the key problem of working within a predetermined word length was noted in an earlier chapter – but a dissertation can pose particular problems if you have never before had to make decisions for yourself about the kind of topic to be investigated and the remit of that topic.

Time and resources

It is important that you make realistic decisions about the time and the resources that you have available for the task that you are designing. In particular, you need to consider any limits on the duration of your study. If your proposed study involves some action on your part (especially action that is an intervention in an aspect of the normal professional process) then you will need to recognize that measured action takes time to devise, test, put into effect and, importantly, may need to take place consistently over a substantial period if any effects are to be identifiable or measurable.

Ethical boundaries

The kind of study that you engage in at dissertation level is likely to have an investigative component which may carry ethical implications; there is therefore a need for you to consider the parameters of the study in terms of any ethical considerations. These considerations might range from the ethics of business management, through relationships with clients, privileged knowledge, and environmental issues, to animal rights. In some cases, such as the professions allied to medicine, ethical concerns will feature prominently in preliminary considerations of what kind of investigation is possible. Your professional body may have a set of guidelines relevant to your circumstances.

Many studies involve the use of human subjects in one way or another: in participating in interviews, psychological tests or drugs trials or in completing questionnaires. By way of an example, the following is a selection of the issues you may need to consider in any project involving human subjects:

- the basic need to ensure that no harm of any kind comes to people as a result of their participation in your investigation;
- the consent of your subjects to taking part, and its possible withdrawal (this can be a particularly sensitive matter if you are dealing with people who may have difficulty in giving informed consent, such as individuals with learning difficulties);
- difficulties that arise whenever there is any deliberate deception in your investigation – for example, where you intend not to tell subjects why you are asking your questions (many would consider any such deliberate deception unethical);
- debriefing of subjects and dealing with and difficulties that arise;

- maintaining the confidentiality of any information given to you by subjects, respecting the privacy of any participants in your investigation and generally protecting them from any harm that might arise from your questioning or from your results;
- resolving tensions between your professional duty to intervene in a situation and your need, for the purposes of your study, simply to act as an observer.

Need to generalize findings

A key issue to be considered at the planning stage of your dissertation is whether or not there is a need for your findings to be generalizable. If you need to show not only that something happens under a set of circumstances but also that the same thing is likely to happen under other similar but different circumstances, then your task takes on a new dimension which requires that you pay particular attention to the way in which you set up your study. For example, you will need to consider the sample or the situation that you investigate to ensure that it is in some way representative: is the group of pregnant women you have interviewed about their diet representative of all women everywhere? The finer points of a need for generalizability need pursuing in the context of your disciplinary area, suffice it to say here that *if* generalizability is required of your dissertation then you will be constrained in terms of the question(s) you pursue as well as the sample you investigate, your method of gathering data and the way in which you analyse your results. This is not to suggest that generalizability of findings *is* necessary or even desirable: the study of pregnant women could be valid even if your sample included a high proportion from a defined ethnic subgroup, or a particular age group or a particular geographic area which has its own dietary customs – what is important is that you recognize the nature of your sample for what it is and make claims that address that nature.

Need to isolate factors

Another constraining dimension is the degree to which your study is required to isolate factors within the setting under investigation.

It may be that central to your research question is the need to focus on one aspect of a complex situation and to separate it out from other factors or interactions (for example, to isolate the genetic component in the development of a physical condition that is also affected by environmental factors or to isolate the role a particular kind of fish plays in a developing ecosystem). To do this requires a particular kind of design in which controlling the variables and eliminating, as far as possible, confounding factors becomes paramount. This is in contrast to the kind of study (for example, a study of bereavement in a particular culture in which changing attitudes to death as a result of cross-cultural influences conflict with accepted practices and rituals) where it is precisely the interaction of all the factors in the given context that is of interest: in this latter case to separate out one feature for examination in isolation from the other factors would be self-defeating.

Academic insularity

Finally, in terms of constraints, there is the possibility that a strong departmental ethos within your university may act to confine rather than liberate your studies because it gives credence to one kind of view or methodology to the exclusion of others. In a spirit of academic freedom different conflicting views should be welcomed, but in a less than perfect world this is not always the case.

Of course it is perfectly reasonable for a university, or more likely departmental, ethos to exist; indeed, you may have been attracted to your academic institution because it promulgates a particular set of beliefs with which you tend to concur. But there is an ever present danger of a shared view (of the kinds of question that are worth asking as well as of the kinds of methodologies used to answer them) becoming the dominant and then the exclusive view. If this happens then the resulting ideological narrowness can be a problem for you as a student. On the one hand, you are vulnerable to a kind of assessment procedure in which a prevailing view is likely to hold sway; on the other hand, you have returned to study, in part at least, to broaden your mind and actively to take on different perspectives rather than simply absorb a set of dictates in the form of an accepted wisdom.

If you are to avoid your dissertation being confined by any particular set of ideological beliefs then it will help if you can read opposing views on issues and on the appropriateness of differing methodologies. The system of external validation of course design and assessment which is central to academia in the UK operates as a set of checks and balances to ensure intellectual openness, and in the final analysis it is worth pinning your faith on that system.

Some of the issues considered above are discussed more fully in Mullarkey (1993).

Writing a dissertation title

We said earlier in this chapter that the question underpinning your dissertation is more likely to be determined by you than by your tutor. The same is also likely to be true of the title of your work. Experience has shown that this is no trivial matter. Indeed, dissertation titles are often a bone of contention at the final examination stage when it is fairly common for examiners to complain about over-long, misleading or opaque titles.

A title needs to be succinct yet unambiguous. A useful start in composing a title is to set down the words that you think encompass what the work is about (the keywords). You then pare down these initial words until you have a list that contains only those which are essential for an understanding to be gained by your reader. Then it is a matter of arranging those words into a form that is grammatically correct and which conveys the message of the work appropriately. You need to avoid both titles that are so short as to become opaque and titles that are so long as to be cumbersome. Suppose, for example, that your dissertation is about how the North Sea has been affected by industrial pollution. Here are some possible titles:

- 'How the North Sea has been affected by industrial pollution': a poor title because it sounds too general.
- 'Industrial pollution': a poor title because the subject matter is not clearly defined.
- 'Industrial pollution in the North Sea': a weak title because it could relate to a number of topics (how the waste came to be

in the North Sea, how to get rid of it, whether or not it is there in significant amounts).
• 'Industrial pollution haunts North Sea users': an inappropriate title because it is more akin to what is required in journalism than academia; it is not related directly to the topic and includes words that might mislead ('haunts' is not used in its proper sense and 'users' is ill defined).
• 'An investigation into the long-term and short-term effects of any leakage of Industrial Pollution into the North Sea': a title that is much too long; the first three words are redundant (and will almost always be so in any dissertation title because it is accepted that an investigation is involved) and the distinction between long-term and short-term effects is all-encompassing and therefore meaningless.
• 'The effects of industrial pollution in the North Sea': a good title because it is understandable and summarizes the content without redundant words.

Writing an abstract

The use of an abstract was advocated in Chapter 5 as a useful summary of content before the reader begins the main part of the text. In a dissertation an abstract is likely to be a *requirement* and therefore deserves special attention here.

An abstract is a self-contained synopsis of a piece of work. It is presented at the beginning of the work, though it will usually be the last thing to be written. It is necessarily short, typically around 200 words, and should contain:

• a description of the main activity of the study;
• a description of the scope of the work;
• a brief outline of the methodology, where necessary, to convey in broad terms what was done and why (for example, it might be necessary to state that a particular experimental design had been used so that the reader can understand the significance and the limitations of results);
• an outline of the most important results, outcomes or findings of the study;

- a summary statement of any conclusions or recommendations that can be made.

It should not go into any details or qualifications or elaboration on these points. It is intended to force home the critical issues of the study rather than analyse the content.

You may recall that we looked briefly at an example of an abstract (from Atkinson 1988). We now return to that example in order to deconstruct it in the terms of the requirements just listed above:

- The main activity of the study: *'The intention of this article is to examine three strands of research concerning the relationship between pupil cognitive style (as assessed by the Cognitive Styles Analysis) and the following factors: pupil performance in GCSE technology examination project work; teaching strategy; teacher and pupil motivation.'*
- The scope of the work: *'The research was investigated with a sample of 112 15–16-year-old pupils (85 boys and 27 girls) selected from eight schools.'*
- A brief outline of the methodology: (this is not present in this exemplar; given where it was published, such as outline was probably not necessary).
- An outline of the most important results, outcomes or findings of the study: *'Analysis of the data collected indicated that a pupil's cognitive style did affect their ability to perform in GCSE design and technology project work.'*
- A summary statement of any conclusions or recommendations that can be made: *'The teaching strategy adopted was shown to have differing effects upon a pupil's performance depending upon the cognitive style of that pupil. The data also indicated that the relationship between a pupil's motivation and their teacher's motivation was affected by a pupil's cognitive style.'*

Supervisory feedback

The writing of a dissertation or final report usually involves a longer period of time and more one-to-one supervision than does any previous work in a programme of study. There should, therefore, be opportunity for you to receive feedback as you undergo the process of planning, investigating and writing up the work (rather than only after completion). Let us therefore consider how to make use of this feedback.

Proactively seeking advice

As you progress through the investigation of issues and the writing of the dissertation itself, so the kind of advice you will require changes. You need to recognize this and actively seek the appropriate kind of feedback at the right time. In my experience some students are very good at getting the most out of me as a supervisor and varying their questioning as they progress; others are less so and tend to remain at one level where they either expect too much or too little or an inappropriate kind of guidance.

To get the best out of your supervisor, you need to see yourself as managing the way in which you are being supervised:

- At the early stages of the dissertation period you need to ask for guidance on the questions that you are asking (for example, 'is my underlying question reasonable and likely to produce useful results?').
- Subsequently, you need to ask for advice on methods of data collection, experimental procedures or literature searching ('how do I go about finding out if the new approach advocated by some in the field is actually delivering the kind of better industrial relations claimed?').
- Then you will need to be asking questions about the progress of any 'fieldwork' and about how you may need to shift the focus of your work according to the kinds of findings that you are getting ('the interviews I conducted have raised some unexpected questions – should I pursue them or should I stay with the original plan and write up what I have got?').
- Finally, you will need to ask questions about the presentation of your work: where to use a diagrammatic form, what material should be in an appendix, how to use references and footnotes ('one of the interviews in particular was fascinating – could I put the whole of the transcript in the main body of the text or should I leave it in the appendix with the rest and just quote odd sentences').

Your expectations of your supervisor

One thing that grieves many of my colleagues is that some of their students expect them to read material full of grammatical and spelling errors, or otherwise poorly presented, with a view to offering constructive guidance for redrafting. Poor presentation, of whatever kind and for whatever reason, obscures meaning and takes up the supervisor's valuable time – apart from which, dealing with matters of this kind is hardly the best use of the supervisor's skills and expertise. It is a relatively straightforward matter to tidy up your work by running it through a spell checker (always bearing in mind the reservations expressed about these in Chapter 6) and by reading it through.

Supervisors are there to offer guidance and suggestions. They will not necessarily insist that you follow their advice to the letter. However, if you do feel that you want to reject your supervisor's advice then you might do well to examine your motives with care. While your own instincts about the best way forward may be rooted quite reasonably, for example, in your professional understanding, the requirements of the dissertation may differ. Your supervisor may help you to interpret the task of writing a dissertation in the context of the intended audience (examiners and others in the field), the assessment procedure (awarding marks according to criteria) and limits and possibilities (the constraining features of the situation, mentioned earlier).

The intricacies of supervisor relationships are discussed thoroughly in the research degree context by Phillips and Pugh (1994) and Cryer (1996). However, do not be put off reading these books just because you are doing a taught course rather than a research degree – much of what these authors say can also be interpreted usefully at the dissertation stage of a taught degree.

Using graphics

Your dissertation or final report might become a very complex as well as lengthy piece of work and because of this you may find it useful to employ graphical representation of one kind or another to simplify ideas, to describe a mass of material succinctly or to give your reader access to large amounts of data at a glance. For example, you might use:

- pictographs or flowcharts to describe organizations, processes, and cause and effect relationships (for example, the way in which energy is distributed throughout an engineering process);
- graphs to compare and contrast features within the context of the study or describe changes in the state of phenomena (for example, the different scores gained by subjects over a period of time covering a series of different interventions);
- schematic illustrations to describe an operational procedure (for example, the different roles played by participants in an emergency planning scenario).

Sides (1992) gives good advice for those presenting technical or scientific data.

Summary

In this chapter you should have:

- come to a clearer understanding about the purpose behind the kinds of investigation that typically form the final stages of your programme of study;
- thought about the kinds of questions that you might engage in asking and answering;
- learnt about the need for focusing;
- considered the kinds of constraint that are likely to operate on your investigation and on your writing up;
- thought about the relationship between your professional practice and the dissertation stage;
- given some thought to the title and the abstract of your study;
- thought about how to get the most out of your supervisor.

Conclusion

A good dissertation is one in which there is evidence of a clear rationale underpinning a thorough investigation (be it of a philosophical or empirical kind) resulting in correctly interpreted results, all reported accurately and concisely. An excellent dissertation, however, will contain all of these things but will offer in addition an ongoing reflective discourse on the way in which the learner him/herself has been affected by the process of the study. Camus might not have been thinking of 'returning students' when he wrote of the mind watching itself, but his maxim may be none the less useful. A lot of what has been said in this chapter about the development of ideas, working within constraints and so on needs to be made explicit in the way in which you write up your work.

8

 # Conclusion

'Cheshire Puss,' she began, rather timidly . . . 'Would you tell me,
  please, which way I ought to go from here?'
'That depends a good deal on where you want to get to,' said the Cat.
'I don't much care where—', said Alice.
'Then it doesn't matter which way you go,' said the Cat.
                                 (Lewis Carroll, *Alice in Wonderland*)

Overview

In this chapter we draw together the various strands running
through this book and come full circle back to the issue of
personal interpretations of returning to study in particular
and ways of learning in general that were raised in the first
two chapters. We will consider:

- your reasons for returning to study in the context of needing to persevere with your studies in the face of possible
  difficulties;
- the way in which rates of progress in academic study are
  likely to vary;
- the concept of reflective practice;
- the issue of taking risks in academic study.

Introduction

Advice as to the direction to be taken is dependent on where the
questioner wishes to go, as the Cheshire Cat is at pains to point

out to Alice. Similarly, as a student returning to study, it is important for you to develop an understanding of where you want your studying to lead. Seeking strategies to maintain your progress and making use of the various kinds of available support are all contingent upon your goals. It may be an over-simplification to suggest that you are engaging with your current or proposed course of study because you need further professional qualifications. While such things may be driving your decision at one level there may well be a variety of reasons, both personal and professional, that also come into the equation and an honest appraisal of all of your goals and the way in which they interrelate may help you in managing your study effectively.

On the other hand, you may have entered study with no fixed goals, just for the sake of the experience and with an open agenda (though, of course, an openness to new experiences and thus to change becomes an agenda in itself). This is a perfectly respectable position and, of course, entitles you to be less directive in the ways in which you monitor your progress and develop strategies.

Maintaining focus in the face of risk and variable progress

Perseverance

It is sobering to recognize that a proportion of students who return to study do not complete their chosen programme of work for one reason or another. Indeed, it is likely that more than one reason will combine in individual cases to provoke lack of completion. In my experience of professionals returning to study, it is typically the case that those who do not succeed will themselves have decided to withdraw rather than failed through any process of assessment. This is not to suggest, of course, that only those prepared to persevere will succeed, but rather that there are features in life that may conspire to foil an honest and enthusiastic attempt at returning to study. It would be facile to try to list here the aspects of your personal and/or professional life that might affect your progress significantly; suffice it to say that they exist for the vast majority of returning students. It may be opportune for you to think back to Chapter 1, when you were asked to consider your reasons for returning to study. Some of my students have found that when they have needed to take difficult decisions – as a result of various life changes, for example – they have had to strike a balance between the continuing relevance of their initial reasons and conflicts that have arisen during their time of studying.

Of course, an alternative approach to the above notions of perseverance would be to follow the advice (not recommended here but noted anyway) of W.C. Fields: 'If at first you don't succeed, try, try, again. Then quit. No use being a damned fool about it.'

Risk taking

When you choose assignment titles and design projects it is sometimes the case that you are more likely to make gains (both in terms of your professional knowledge and expertise and assignment grade) if you take a little risk. For example, it may be that choosing an area with which you are *not* familiar will bring more gain in terms of extending your knowledge base than choosing the familiar but safe; similarly, it may be that choosing to undertake an investigatory project which involves the testing of innovatory materials or procedures is of more potential value than replicating existing studies of common features of professional life. Clearly, however, the very nature of risk taking is that it is accompanied by the prospect of failure at one level or another. It would be helpful, if you can, to talk through with your supervisor at the outset the kinds of result that are likely to accrue from your choice of topic or title. Typically, in academic study, it is not so much the result that matters as the way in which you ask the question. In other words there may be no such thing as a 'failed' investigation in your area if that investigation is based on sound, rational questions, is carried out according to appropriate practices and if the results are analysed according to relevant criteria. In this sense, a 'negative' result should always tell you as the investigator something. In any case, genuinely important questions often involve some measure of risk in one form or another.

Rate of progress

Many students grow frustrated when progress on a piece of work, or on the course of their studies as a whole, seems to them to be unnaturally slow. Yet it needs to be recognized that the rate of progress in academic studies will tend to be irregular. You will often find yourself spending a great deal of time mastering a particular technique or reading around a topic before your efforts begin to produce results. This may be in stark contrast to

---

 Reflection: Rates of progress

Can you think of examples from your previous experiences of study, or from your current professional practice, in which there has been a significant amount of time and effort expended before any real gains in terms of production or of new learning of knowledge or skills? How justifiable does the time and effort seem now, in retrospect?

 Student responses

I do a lot of background work before finalizing suggestions on a project. It is still a necessary expense of time, although I am better now at judging how complex a presentation a client needs. Without the background work a project is likely to lack depth – in some ways I hate to work on things that won't really feature in the final presentation but at the same time I know it is necessary. I guess it's the same with academic work although I confess that there I am likely to plunge in without the background. Maybe I need to learn a lesson.

(Designer)

I spent ages getting into using databases etc. on the computer – but it was worth it in the end, it has opened up lots of possibilities. I'm pretty sure I wouldn't be getting the kind of grades I get now without that initial work.

(Secondary school teacher)

your professional work, where the relationship between effort and progress seems more regular and therefore more predictable. Frequently it is the unfamiliarity of rate of progress in academic work that can be unnerving for a professional returning to study, and you may have to rationalize what is happening in this respect.

The reflective practitioner

Yours may be one of the many professions which make use of the concept of the 'reflective practitioner'. As professions have developed and as society has become more complex, the notion of a set body of knowledge, learnt once and adequate for the purpose throughout a career, has changed. It is likely that, as a professional, you need to see yourself as both working at your practice and improving your skills and enhancing your knowledge base within that practice. In many ways it may no longer be good enough to be able to perform at an adequate level of professional practice in the here and now – you may also have to monitor continuously your professional process with a view to improvement.

The extent to which this applies will vary across professions, but there is no doubt that the concept of the reflective practitioner has influenced the way in which many courses which relate to professional development are taught and assessed. Typically, issues within professional practice which need to be investigated and evaluated are identified, ways of systematically analysing practice are explored and the implications of any modifications to that practice are discussed. Students are encouraged to make changes in their professional practice based on reasoned argument and evidence which result in a 'better' situation (you may wish to reflect on what could count as 'better' in your own professional context, though one could argue that it should, in one way or another, relate ultimately to improvement for the client group). Of course such improvement is cyclical: change will bring about circumstances which in themselves need to be open to scrutiny and so the cycle of reflection and change will continue.

Seeking support and dealing with self-doubt

Support from others

As you return to study you may feel you are in an isolated position. Yet, it is worth remembering that most of your friends and colleagues will want you to succeed in your studies. Therefore, you may be able to reduce the feeling of isolation by reviewing your own situation with regard to support:

- Family and friends may be invaluable in terms of motivation and perseverance.
- Professional colleagues may be able to provide expertise and knowledge as well as practical help in the form of, for example, case material.
- Tutors within the academic setting should be able to motivate, for example, by helping you to structure your work.

Support from supplementary reading

Throughout this book I have mentioned sources in the literature where you may find help on certain issues and this is perhaps the moment to draw your attention again to the References and Suggestions for Further Reading at the back of the book. In general terms, books such as Race (1998), Marshall and Rowland (1993) and Northedge (1990) all offer excellent advice and guidance. More specifically, hooks (1994) and Mezirow (1990) might be helpful in that they offer challenging views on what education is in the wider sense and by implication what study might be about in the narrower sense.

Accepting uncertainty

It would be glib to suggest simply that self-doubt is a perfectly normal and acceptable feature of returning to study. Doubting one's own abilities can be a destructive force if, for example, it results in a concentration on defence against perceived threat rather than a focus on learning. But self-doubt is common among students returning to study – and, indeed, it is prevalent among many of those who spend the majority of their professional lives within academia. When you engage in study, you necessarily challenge yourself and your beliefs; with that challenge come the attendant risks of doubting your beliefs, your knowledge systems and the effectiveness of your professional skills. In short, constant critical evaluation of your own professional practice can seem inevitably to provoke uncertainty. But returning to study should be an enriching and a life-enhancing experience. While it may be uncomfortable, uncertainty is a more natural, and ultimately more beneficial, state of mind than certainty.

Summary

This chapter has considered personal interpretations of returning to study and ways of learning.

- We have looked again at reasons for returning to study.
- We have addressed the way in which rates of progress in academic study are likely to vary.
- We have considered the concept of the reflective practitioner.
- We have considered possible sources of support.
- We have identified the inevitability of taking risks in academic study.

Conclusion

There is a tension of sorts between the way the words of Lewis Carroll are employed at the outset of this chapter, and the kind of acceptance of uncertainty advocated at the end. On the one hand, the usefulness of knowing where you are going is stressed and yet on the other the foolhardiness of accepting certainty is underlined. How, then, can we reconcile the need for a clear sense of direction with a rejection of certainty? You must define for yourself the personal and professional goals that you wish to attain. The exciting thing about returning to study is that it gives you the opportunity to challenge accepted views and rethink your own ideas and motivations as well as to develop your professional knowledge and skills and your personal abilities as a thinker and a learner. If reading this book helps you to take that opportunity and exploit it to the full, then the book will have served its purpose.

References

Allison, D. and Bramwell, N. (1994) It'll be all right on the day, *Biologist*, 41, 4.

Atkinson, S. (1998) Cognitive style in the context of design and technology project work, *Educational Psychology*, 18(2), 183–94.

Beddows, C. (1989) *Returning to Study*. London: Heinemann.

Bell, J. (1993) *Doing Your Research Project: A Guide for First-Time Researchers in Education and Social Science*, 2nd edn. Buckingham: Open University Press.

Brockbank, A. and McGill, I. (1998) *Facilitating Reflective Learning in Higher Education*. Buckingham: Society for Research into Higher Education/ Open University Press.

Burgess, R.G. (1997) *Beyond the First Degree: Graduate Education, Lifelong Learning and Careers*. Buckingham: Society for Research into Higher Education/Open University Press.

Collinson, D., Kirkup, G., Kyd, R. and Slocombe, L. (1992) *Plain English*. Buckingham: Open University Press.

Creme, P. and Lea, M.R. (1997) *Writing at University: A Guide for Students*. Buckingham: Open University Press.

Cryer, P. (1996) *The Research Student's Guide to Success*. Buckingham: Open University Press.

Dane, F.C. (1990) *Research Methods*. Pacific Grove, CA: Brooks/Cole.

Denscombe, M. (1998) *The Good Research Guide: for Small-Scale Social Research Projects*. Buckingham: Open University Press.

Fairbairn, G.J. and Winch, C. (1996) *Reading, Writing and Reasoning: A Guide for Students*, 2nd edn. Buckingham: Open University Press.

Fowler, H.W. (1990) *Modern English Usage*, 2nd edn. Oxford: Oxford University Press.

Hall, C. (1994) *Getting Down to Writing – a Student's Guide to Overcoming Writer's Block*. Dereham, Norfolk: Peter Francis Publishers (on behalf of the Centre for Research into Human Communication and Learning, Cambridge).

Halpern, D.F. (1984) *Thought and Knowledge – An Introduction to Critical Thinking*. Hillsdale, NJ: Lawrence Erlbaum Associates.

Hamp-Lyons, L. and Courter, K.B. (1984) *Research Matters*. New York: Harper & Row.

Hampson, L. (1994) *How's Your Dissertation Going?* Lancaster: Unit for Innovation in Higher Education.

Hardie, E.T.L. and Neou, V. (eds) (1994) *Internet: Mailing Lists*. Englewood Cliffs, NJ: Prentice Hall.

Harmon, C. (ed.) (1996) *Using the Internet, On-line Services and CD-ROMs for Writing Research and Term Papers*. New York: Neal-Schuman Publishers.

hooks, b. (1994) *Teaching to Transgress: Education as the Practice of Freedom*. New York: Routledge.

Marshall, L. and Rowland, F. (1993) *A Guide to Learning Independently*, 2nd edn. Buckingham: Open University Press.

Mezirow, J. (1990) *Fostering Critical Reflection in Adulthood: A Guide to Transformative and Emancipatory Learning*. San Francisco: Jossey-Bass.

Miller, C. and Swift, K. (1989) *The Handbook of Non-sexist Writing: For Writers, Editors and Speakers*, 2nd edn. London: Women's Press.

Mullarkey, N. (1993) *You Do Not Seem to Have Understood the Question*. Lancaster: University of Lancaster Press.

Nietzsche, F. (1968) *The Will to Power*. New York: Vintage Books.

Norris, J.R. (1978) How to give a research talk: notes for inexperienced lecturers, *Biologist*, 25, 68–74.

Northedge, A. (1990) *The Good Study Guide*. Milton Keynes: Open University Educational Enterprises.

Parnes, S.J., Noller, R.B., and Biondi, A.M. (1977) *Guide to Creative Action: Revised Edition of Creative Behavior Guidebook*. New York: Scribner.

Phelan, P.D. and Reynolds, P. (1995) *Argument and Evidence: Critical Thinking for the Social Sciences*. London: Routledge.

Phillips, E.M. and Pugh, D.S. (1994) *How to Get a PhD*, 2nd edn. Buckingham: Open University Press.

Race, P. (1999) *How to Get a Good Degree: Making the Most of Your Time at University*. Buckingham: Open University Press.

Rowntree, D. (1988) *Learn How to Study*. London: Macdonald Orbis.

Seal, B. (1997) *Academic Encounters: Reading, Study Skills, and Writing*. Cambridge: Cambridge University Press.

Sides, C.H. (1992) *How to Write and Present Technical Information*, 2nd edn. Cambridge: Cambridge University Press.

Torrance, M.S. and Thomas, G.V. (1994) The development of writing skills in doctoral research students, in R.G. Burgess (ed.) *Postgraduate Education and Training in the Social Sciences – Processes and Products*. London: Jessica Kingsley.

Weissberg, R. and Buker, S. (1990) *Writing up Research – Experimental Research Report Writing for Students of English*. Englewood Cliffs, NJ: Prentice Hall.

Suggestions for further reading

I have noted below some books and articles that I think may prove useful in your return to study. I have included some texts that are directed at supervisors on the grounds that they inform the general debate about engaging in advanced study.

General study guides

Arksey, H., Marchant, I. and Simmill, C. (1994) *Juggling for a Degree – Mature Students' Experience of University Life*. Lancaster: Unit for Innovation in Higher Education.

Beddows, C. (1989) *Returning to Study*. London: Heinemann.

Hampson, L. (1994) *How's Your Dissertation Going?* Lancaster: Unit for Innovation in Higher Education.

Marshall, L. and Rowland, F. (1993) *A Guide to Learning Independently*, 2nd edn. Buckingham: Open University Press.

Mullarkey, N. (1993) *You Do Not Seem to Have Understood the Question*. Lancaster: University of Lancaster Press.

Northedge, A. (1990) *The Good Study Guide*. Milton Keynes: The Open University.

Raaheim, K., Wankowski, J. and Radford, J. (1991) *Helping Students to Learn: Teaching, Counselling, Research*. Buckingham: Society for Research into Higher Education/Open University Press.

Race, P. (1999) *How to Get a Good Degree: Making the Most of Your Time at University*. Buckingham: Open University Press.

Rickards, T. (1992) *How to Win as a Mature Student.* London: Kogan Page.
Rowntree, D. (1988) *Learn How to Study.* London: Macdonald Orbis.
Smith, B.R. (1983) Learning difficulties of part-time mature students, *Journal of Further and Higher Education,* 7, 81–5.

Academic writing (general)

Baker, S. (1989) *The Practical Stylist,* 7th edn. New York: Harper & Row.
Collinson, D., Kirkup, G., Kyd, R. and Slocombe, L. (1992) *Plain English.* Buckingham: Open University Press.
Creme, P. and Lea, M.R. (1997) *Writing at University : A Guide for Students.* Buckingham: Open University Press.
Fairbairn, G.J. and Winch, C. (1996) *Reading, Writing and Reasoning: A Guide for Students,* 2nd edn. Buckingham: Open University Press.
Fowler, H.W. (1990) *Modern English Usage,* 2nd edn. Oxford: Oxford University Press.
Hall, C. (1994) *Getting Down to Writing – A Student's Guide to Over-coming Writer's Block.* Dereham: Peter Francis Publishers, on behalf of the Centre for Research into Human Communication and Learning, Cambridge.
Miller, C. and Swift, K. (1989) *The Handbook of Non-sexist Writing: For Writers, Editors and Speakers,* 2nd edn. London: Women's Press.
Seal, B. (1997) *Academic Encounters: Reading, Study skills, and Writing.* Cambridge: Cambridge University Press.
Swales, J. (1990) *Genre Analysis – English in Academic and Research Settings.* New York: Cambridge University Press.
Swales, J.M. and Feak, C.B. (1994) *Academic Writing for Graduate Students.* Ann Arbor: University of Michigan Press.
Trezeciak, J. and Mackay, S.E. (1994) *Study Skills for Academic Writing.* Hemel Hempstead: Prentice Hall.

Academic writing (scientific/technical)

Booth, V. (1993) *Communicating in Science – Writing a Scientific Paper and Speaking at Scientific Meetings,* 2nd edn. Cambridge: Cambridge University Press.
Day, R.A. (1989) *How to Write and Publish a Scientific Paper,* 3rd edn. Cambridge: Cambridge University Press.
Hers, H.G. (1984) Making science a good read, *Nature,* 307, 205.
Lobban, C.S. and Schefter, M. (1993) *Successful Lab Reports – A Manual for Science Students.* Cambridge: Cambridge University Press.

Sides, C.H. (1992) *How to Write and Present Technical Information*, 2nd edn. Cambridge: Cambridge University Press.

Weissberg, R. and Buker, S. (1990) *Writing up Research – Experimental Research Report Writing for Students of English*. Englewood Cliffs, NJ: Prentice Hall.

Zinsser, W. (1985) *On Writing Well – An Informal Guide to Writing Nonfiction*, 3rd edn. New York: Harper & Row.

Critical thinking

Halpern, D.F. (1984) *Thought and Knowledge – An Introduction to Critical Thinking*. Hillsdale, NJ: Lawrence Erlbaum Associates.

hooks, b. (1994) *Teaching to Transgress: Education as the Practice of Freedom*. New York: Routledge.

Meltzer, M. and Palau, S. (1996) *Acquiring Critical Thinking Skills*. London: W.B. Saunders.

Mezirow, J. (1990) *Fostering Critical Reflection in Adulthood : A Guide to Transformative and Emancipatory Learning*. San Francisco: Jossey-Bass.

Parnes, S.J., Noller, R.B. and Biondi, A.M. (1977) *Guide to Creative Action: Revised Edition of Creative Behavior Guidebook*. New York: Scribner.

Phelan, P.D. and Reynolds, P. (1995) *Argument and Evidence: Critical Thinking for the Social Sciences*. London: Routledge.

Oral presentations

Allison, D. and Bramwell, N. (1994) It'll be all right on the day, *Biologist*, 41, 4.

Norris, J.R. (1978) How to give a research talk: Notes for inexperienced lecturers, *Biologist*, 25, 68–74.

Accessing the Internet

Hardie, E.T.L. and Neou, V. (eds) (1994) *Internet: Mailing Lists*. Englewood Cliffs, NJ: Prentice Hall.

Harmon, C. (ed.) (1996) *Using the Internet, On-line Services & CD-ROMs for Writing Research and Term Papers*. New York: Neal-Schuman Publishers.

For research students

Bell, J. (1993) *Doing Your Research Project: A Guide for First-Time Researchers in Education and Social Science*, 2nd edn. Buckingham: Open University Press.

Blaxter, L., Hughes, C. and Tight, M. (1996) *How to Research*. Buckingham: Open University Press.

Cryer, P. (1996) *The Research Student's Guide to Success*. Buckingham: Open University Press.

Hamp-Lyons, L. and Courter, K.B. (1984) *Research Matters*. New York: Harper & Row.

Major, L.E. (1994) The doctors of debt, doubt and despondency. *Times Higher Education Supplement*, 22 July, 6–7.

Orna, L. with Stevens, G. (1995) *Managing Information for Research*. Buckingham: Open University Press.

Phillips, E.M. and Pugh, D.S. (1994) *How to Get a PhD*, 2nd edn. Buckingham: Open University Press.

Torrance, M.S. and Thomas, G.V. (1994) The development of writing skills in doctoral research students, in R.G. Burgess (ed.), *Postgraduate Education and Training in the Social Sciences – Processes and Products*. London: Jessica Kingsley.

Wright, J. and Lodwick, R. (1989) The process of the PhD: A study of the first year of doctoral study. *Research Papers in Education*, 4, 22–56.

For academic supervisors

Black, D. (1994) *A Guide for Research Supervisors*. Dereham: Peter Francis Publishers on behalf of the Centre for Research into Human Communication and Learning, Cambridge.

Brockbank, A. and McGill, I. (1998) *Facilitating Reflective Learning in Higher Education*. Buckingham: Society for Research into Higher Education / Open University Press.

Hockey, J. (1994) Establishing boundaries: problems and solutions in managing the PhD supervisor's role, *Cambridge Journal of Education*, 24, 293–307.

General issues in higher education

Blaxter, L., Hughes, C. and Tight, M. (1998) *The Academic Career Handbook*. Buckingham: Open University Press.

Burgess, R.G. (1997) *Beyond the First Degree: Graduate Education, Lifelong Learning and Careers.* Buckingham: Society for Research into Higher Education/Open University Press.

Neal, S. (1998) *The Making of Equal Opportunities Policies in Universities.* Buckingham: Society for Research into Higher Education/Open University Press.

Smith, A. and Webster, F. (eds) (1997) *The Postmodern University?* Buckingham: Open University Press.

Index